THE EXPERIENCE

FATIMA L. MASSEY

THE EXPERIENCE

@Copyright 2020 by Fatima L. Massey

All rights reserved. No part of this book maybe reproduced or transmitted in any form or by any means without prior written permission from the author.

ISBN: 978-1-953638-02-1

Printed in the United States of America

This book or parts thereof may not be reproduced in any form, stored in a retrieval system, or transmitted in any form by any means-electronic, mechanical, photocopy, recording, or otherwise-without prior written permission of the publisher, except as provided by United States of America copyright law.

PUBLISHER
TA MEDIA & PRODUCTIONS LLC
DALLAS, TX 75240
www.PUBLISHYOURBOOKTODAY.INFO
WWW.TAMEDIACO.COM

IMAGE ON COVER (Castle Berry Productions)

Unless otherwise noted, all Scripture quotations are taken from the Holy Bible, King James Version
(PUBLIC DOMAIN PER BIBLEGATEWAY.COM)

Holy Bible, New International Version®, NIV® Copyright ©1973, 1978, 1984, 2011 by Biblica, Inc.® Used by permission. All rights reserved worldwide.

The Holy Bible, English Standard Version. ESV® Text Edition: 2016. Copyright © 2001 by Crossway Bibles, a publishing ministry of Good News Publishers

LOVE + APPRECIATION

I would like to give honor to God, my Lord and Savior Jesus Christ. Who is the keeper of my soul? I find Shalom (peace) within when I seek you.

I would like to thank my squad. My lovely children, Brian Richardson and Faith Smith for being my rough riders through this entire journey. This was not only an experience for me but for them as well. You both stood firm through our ups and downs. Thank you for trusting the process.

The third squad member is my mom Belivia Ridgell. There is so much I can say about this lady. But I will sum it all up with the word love. Your love is beyond measure. Thank you, mom, for being my biggest supporter.

Love and blessings to all my family, friends and clients.

Thanks to all the Faith Sister supports who purchased my first book.

ENCOURAGEMENT FOR GOD'S BELOVED

If this is your first time reading a book written by me, I want to share something with you. I had been in a place where God allowed me to hear directly from Him to receive direction. I was allowing myself to be led by the Holy Spirit/ the Spirit of God inside of me. No one prophesied to me or told me what they heard the Lord said to them for me. The Lord told me He wanted me to become familiar with hearing from Him. Hearing from God is a gift and I enjoy it. I had to sit quietly, alone and still. Even if I had to learn through trial and error, it was my journey and my walk with God. So, I want you to know that it's ok to experience this walk alone especially in the early stage of getting to know God. In your time of being alone you can pray, read (the word of God) and worship to become familiar with the leading of the Holy One.

A MESSAGE FOR GOD'S BELOVED

Jeremiah 29:11 says, "For I know the thoughts that I think toward you, saith the Lord, thoughts of peace, and not of evil, to give you an expected end".

Beloved, God already has plans for you. Which means it's already done and established. His plans are not grievous but of peace. That means no chaos or confusion. His plans are not deceiving. He says, His plans are not evil. Which means, He doesn't want to bring any harm toward you with the plans He has established for you. His thoughts and plans will give you an expected end. That means, "Something has to happen". There's no if, and, or, but to God's plan. There is a result to the matter. A result is an outcome, the conclusion of a situation or matter. Don't you want to see the outcome to God's plan for your life? Our God thinks big. He is the Almighty One. His thoughts are higher than we can imagine.

Isaiah 55:8,9 says, "For my thoughts are not your thoughts and neither are my ways your ways, saith the Lord. For as the heavens are higher than the earth, so are my ways higher than your ways and my thoughts your thoughts".

Beloved, God's ways are much greater than our ways. Sometimes the way we want to do things is below average. They are below God's standards and expectations for us. God's expectations are all the way up. We must step our game up as kingdom believers. Get on God's level. God's thoughts are in the heavens.

Psalm 24:3 says it perfectly, "Who can ascend into the hill of the Lord, who can stand in His holy place".

That's where our thoughts should come from. That place of holy, in heaven, from the Holy One. You do know, we are made in the image of God. So, Beloved, since we are made like Him, we should think like Him. Because we receive our thoughts from H

TABLE OF CONTENTS

INTRODUCTION 1
WILDERNESS DETOUR 5

CHAPTER ONE
IT DON'T ALWAYS GO AS YOU PLAN **8**

CHAPTER TWO
ON TO THE NEXT **15**

CHAPTER THREE
LEAVE THY KINDRED **18**

CHAPTER FOUR
THE SAN DIEGO EXPERIENCE **23**

CHAPTER FIVE
PEOPLE TEST YOU **30**

CHAPTER SIX
THE DREAM CENTER EXPERIENCE **36**

CHAPTER SEVEN
THE LA EXPERIENCE **44**

CHAPTER EIGHT
JUST A LITTLE REST IN ENCINO **51**

CHAPTER NINE
THE INGLEWOOD EXPERIENCE **57**

CHAPTER TEN
THE REDONDO BEACH EXPERIENCE **68**

CHAPTER ELEVEN
THE PASADENA EXPERIENCE **80**

CHAPTER TWELVE
THE HEART AND SOUL OF A REALTOR **90**

CHAPTER THIRTEEN
JUST IN TIME **96**

CHAPTER FOURTEEN
THE SLIGHT MISSED OPPORTUNITY **99**

CHAPTER FIFTHTEEN
THE DOOR OF HOPE EXPERIENCE **103**

CHAPTER SIXTEEN
HALLELUJAH WE ARE FREE **111**

CHAPTER SEVENTEEN
A CALL TO MINISTRY **115**

CHAPTER EIGHTEEN
ORDINATION **121**

CHAPTER NINETEEN
BYE BYE CALI, SWEET HOME CHICAGO **124**

ENCOURAGEMENT FOR GOD'S BELOVED 127

INTRODUCTION

I am away on a 10-15-day Sabbatical. Quite exhausted from life. Not where I thought I should be in life by now. God is sustaining me. Some days I'm up and some days I'm feeling down. But that's a part of being a human being with emotions. As much as I like to look at myself as Wonder Woman (at least that's who I thought I was as a kid), I am not her. I can't solve every problem all the time. I walk by faith. Even that can get very tiring in this journey the Lord has taken me on.

In my last book I shared how the Lord was directing my path. He took me on a journey, a walk of faith, being led by the Holy Spirit/The Spirit of God. In the very beginning I was so excited as I was hearing and obeying the instructions from the Lord. Waiting for the next move after the next move. Hoping I was getting closer and closer to, "The Big Plan". Honestly, God hadn't totally shown me the big plan. But I knew, if God was in it, it had to be big and good. So, I kept going. Even though I became exhausted, I knew I wanted to complete my assignment.

Well, I've learned life is a journey and it never stops until we die. So, prepare yourself for the good and the bad experiences that will come your way.

Buckle your seat belt and come along for another roller coaster ride with your Faith Sister, as I share another part of my journey called, "The Experience". While walking in faith, it became very bumpy for me. But as you can see, I am still here. Just know, the walk of faith does not get easy. So, if you are choosing to walk by faith, don't give up. If you give up, what are you going to do? Go back to your old way of living and thinking? That is not an option. We must move forward by all means. For me, it took a lot of crying, praying, worshipping and moving in faith. God kept me. He knew just how much I could handle.

Galatians 6:9 says, "Let us not be weary in well doing, for in due season we shall reap if we faint not".

This book will be very unorthodoxly worded, written, not your ordinary script, grammar sensitive, slang speaking, humorous, exaggeration used, filled with laughter, real, truth, but filled and led by the Holy Spirit/The Spirit of God in me. As I shared this experience, I wanted to be as open as possible. Even if some of the things I was led to do by God seemed crazy.

As you read this book, I want it to feel as if I'm sitting across from you having a conversation, drinking tea and sharing my experiences. It is God's plan for people on all levels of thinking to get an understanding. When I wrote my first book the Lord told me to keep my writing simple. So, that's what I did for this book as well. The Lord wants even our babies to learn to walk in faith, so they too can have their own experience. God Bless and Enjoy!

WILDERNESS DETOUR

During my Journey through California I experienced going through the wilderness, just as Moses and the Israelites experienced. Read below.

Exodus 13:17,18 (NLT Bible Version)

When Pharaoh finally let the people go, God did not lead them along the main road that runs through Philistine territory, even though that was the shortest route to the Promised Land. God said, "If the people are faced with a battle, they might change their minds and return to Egypt."
So, God led them in a roundabout way through the wilderness toward the Red Sea. Thus, the Israelites left Egypt like an army ready for battle.

Exodus 13:21,22 (NLT Bible Version)

The Lord went ahead of them. He guided them during the day with a pillar of cloud, and he provided light at night with a pillar of fire. This allowed them to travel by day or by night.
And the Lord did not remove the pillar of cloud or pillar of fire from its place in front of the people.

God could have taken Moses and the Israelites on a shorter route but that's not what he wanted. Just as he did with me. There were some things God wanted me to experience. In the wilderness God is able to reveal who He is by protecting and providing. His power is demonstrated. In the wilderness God wants us to totally trust in Him. It's where we find trust in Him.

Trust the wilderness.

CHAPTER 1
IT DON'T ALWAYS GO AS YOU PLAN

Life can be so funny. You don't know what direction it will take you. We write our plans down, in hope of it coming to pass. But, when you live a life led by the Spirit of God, sometimes the plans you've written for your life may happen right away, be put on hold or never happen. For those of you who don't know what the Spirit is, it's that instinct you feel inside of you, it's that thought that comes to mind, or (as the word of God says) a still small quiet voice speaking to you, directing your path.

1Kings 19:12 says, "And after the earthquake a fire; but the Lord was not in the fire: and after the fire a still small voice".

I know, hearing those plans being put on hold or never happening sounds sad or disappointing. But it's the truth. I've learned timing is everything. I have also learned from experience that you can believe God for a plan and work hard at pushing that plan. But nothing happened. It was disappointing. But after I saw why it didn't happen, I was thankful to God. Either I didn't need that plan, or it wasn't the right time. There is a purpose and there is a plan for each and every one of us. But it takes life experiences to show us which way to go.

Life experiences are teaching experiences. Even our failing experiences teach us. But you don't know until you step out on faith. I was taken on a roller coaster ride of events during this journey. The name of this roller coaster was called, "The Experience". Some of the things I was led to do looked and sound so crazy. They helped me and the many people involved.

    I had a beautiful home in the South Suburban part of Illinois. I shared in my previous book, how I lived there during a time of what the world called a recession. It was a blessing for me and my children at the time. The mortgage companies were doing modifications. This is when you are on a trial period payment for 3 months. You make a monthly mortgage payment that is much lower than what you normally pay. I always paid my normal monthly payments on time. But I wanted my mortgage lowered because taxes had gone up in my area. The 3 months passed, and the mortgage company decided not to approve me. They wanted me to pay back all the money owed from the previous trial period months and the current mortgage payment. Had I known I wouldn't get approved; I would have kept making my full monthly payments. The bank seemed as if they wanted to help but, it was all a game to them (At least that's what I believe). I went back and forth to court with the bank trying to save my home. My case kept getting prolonged. So, before you know it, I was sitting in my home mortgage free for about two years. I was in hope of keeping my home. That was not part of the plan. I didn't know how or what my kids and I were going to do. I was in a position where I had to, "TRUST GOD".

Proverbs 3:5,6 says, "Trust in the Lord with all thine heart, lean not to thine own understanding. In all thy ways acknowledge Him, and He will direct thy path".

So, we have Fatima, a woman who pays her bills on time, previous salon owner, property owner, a giver, never likes to depend on others for help and carries her own weight (responsibilities). This is a little something about the women you are reading about. But now, she's being placed in a position where she had to learn patience. You can only imagine the turn my life took.

I fought to keep the home and I was believing God to keep us in the home. He kept us in it, but not forever. I was sad and hurt. The mortgage companies were wrong to do people this way. And I just knew God was going to get them for doing one of His believers wrong. God had a different plan for me. So, I had to suck up the pain of leaving my home. It was time to pray, hear and obey the next move God had for me and my family.

I had another property. But I allowed someone to move in assuming she was going to make a purchase. That didn't work out for her because she couldn't get approved. So, I allowed her to pay me a small amount of rent until she didn't want to pay anymore. I knew she didn't have much. Even though I was in need financially, I was still willing to help someone else. I let her know my situation with the property my kids and I were living in before she moved in. I didn't know when the courts would have us leave. So, her staying at my rental property would be a temporary stay for her since she didn't get approved by the bank. I did not do a lease with her. This was more of a, one hand wiping the other situation. Besides, I wasn't paying a mortgage at this property as well. I tell you, God was covering and blessing my children and I, and anyone who was connected to me. This home blessed and sustained families. I remember hearing from God, or I would have a dream letting me know who to allow to live in this home. It was always for a family in need.

The tenant had been staying there for some months. I let the tenant know my children and I will be leaving our home because we finally received the court order and I would need my home she was living in, so we could have a place to live. Now, I didn't just put her out without her having a place to go. She had an option; she just

Well, it seemed as if she was not going to leave. So, there was a little heat between the both of us. I couldn't believe this was happening. Especially since I was nice enough to open my doors to her and she knew the situation coming in. I must admit I was angry. I wanted to go over there and put her out myself. I didn't feel like taking her to court to get her out. I had been through that a few times before with previous tenants. But I clearly heard the Lord say, "Don't fight like that". I kept hearing the words, "Be quiet". Honestly, I was a fireball inside. I wanted to handle this on my own. I've learned (from this experience) doing things God's way, can get things moving quickly and peacefully. The bible speaks about believers handling things outside of court. I did not have the energy to go through another court order with a tenant again.

1 Corinthians 6:1 NIV says, "If any of you has a dispute with another, do you dare to take it before the ungodly (law) for judgement instead or before the Lord's people". She was a believer, a Christian. We as believers should be able to settle our matters outside of court.

I sat quietly, just as the Lord instructed me. I heard nothing from her for days. The Lord must have moved on her heart because she eventually left. I don't remember the exact amount of days, but it was quick. I do remember her texting to let me know she was gone. The house was clean and in order, nothing broken. I was so grateful to God. I thanked her and wished her the best.

What I've learned and what you can learn from each of these experiences are, plans change, don't worry, have patience, be quiet, wait and trust God. Even if a situation looks like it is going in the opposite direction.

I may have wanted to keep my home but that was not what God had in mind. I realize, God already knew how all of this would work out. He knew I would have to leave my home and move into my next property. I did not know I was being prepared to move to California. That's why I still had that rental property. I was mortgage free with the rental property for almost 3 years. I don't know how God worked that deal out but, I am grateful He did.

CHAPTER 2
ON TO THE NEXT

I've learned I live a step by step and moment to moment type of life. The bible speaks of, **"Daily bread", (Matthew 6:11).** I hear to make one move and in obedience I take the step. Then I wait to hear the next move and by faith, I take that step. This is a good way to get in tune with hearing from God. When you make the move there is a result after it. It also keeps us from being anxious about things. **Philippians 4:6 says, "Be anxious for nothing".** We are to pray about everything, every step and every move. Taking those steps can make one impatient, especially when you don't know, but want to see what's on the other side.

My children and I moved into my rental property after having to leave my other home. We stayed there for only a few months. Until it was time to give that home up as well. I did what's called a, "Deed in Lieu" on this property. Which means you voluntarily transfer the title of the property to the lender in exchange for a mortgage release. This was so amazing because as I stated in the previous chapter, I had this home mortgage free for about 3 years. Don't ask me how that happened because I still can't explain. Because I did something called, "Deed in Lieu" on this property, I knew I wouldn't be there long. So, I started selling almost everything I owned. I had a huge garage sale. I also gave away a lot of my big furniture. This was such a sad moment. I had to give up things that were so dear to me. Upon exiting this property, the mortgage company gave me moving money. I felt like I had hit the jackpot because my funds were low. God is so good with the way he strategically makes things work for our good. So, we packed what little belongings we had left in preparation for our next move. And so, our next move was to my mom's place.

I know you are wondering, what's with all this moving around in such a short period of time. Well, in my last book I shared how the Lord was going to move my children and I to California. What I didn't know at the time of all this moving around was God was wrapping up my unfinished business in Illinois, so I could start my journey in California. That's why I was moving from one house to another within an approximately 4month time span. It was a rough summer trying to make ends (money) meet to pay the few bills I had. I was really living a life of faith. Trusting God with every area of my life. My children were young at the time and they found fun in everything. I was in such a serious mode often. Trying to keep my mind at peace so that I could hear from God for the next moves.

CHAPTER 3
LEAVE THY KINDRED

I was exhausted from moving and clearing out two homes. I had things stored at both places. But God gave me strength. Along with a few family members and friends to help me move. I knew I was going to California, but I didn't know when. So, we moved into my mom's place. I registered my kids in school. I was able to rest my mind only for about a month or two after moving.

Then, I clearly heard the Holy Spirit say, "You are going to California". I was in prayer at the time and was excited to hear those words. But then I started thinking about how I just registered my kids for school, and it made no sense to take them out.

So, while in prayer I heard the Spirit say, "You will be leaving your kids here with your mom". You would have thought someone died. I broke down and cried so bad. I didn't want to leave my kids. I needed them with me and they needed me. Besides, they thought they were going to California as well. I knew it would disappoint them to hear they weren't leaving with me.

After using what seemed to be a full roll of tissue, crying my eyes out. I stopped the pity party. I received what the Lord spoke to me. I shared it with my mom, and she was ok with it. She knew this was the plan already, but she hadn't spoken it to me. Sometimes I don't see things until I am in deep prayer with snot and tears. My mom always says to me, "Get out the way". Meaning, get out of God's way so He can take control.

Remember what I said in the beginning of the book how we can have a plan in our head but that may not be the way God wants it to go? Or maybe that plan in our head is on hold for a little while? Well, that's what this plan was all about. My kids were coming with me but not at the very beginning of this journey.

I told my kids God's plan. They were a little sad, but my kids trusted what I was hearing from God. My daughter was excited to be living in the area where my mom stayed because she was closer to her family and friends. My son, on the other hand, is a momma's boy. He and I are in sync. I mentioned in the first book how his dad died and so, I was all he had. I knew me leaving him would be an issue. But he eventually became excited about the plan. The kids and I were thinking I could go there and get established, then send for them. What little did we know.

Time passed and I was sitting around doing nothing at my mom's place. Waiting to hear from God as to when I should leave for California. Well, the Lord spoke. I was reading my bible in the book of Genesis chapter 28 verses 15-17. In the verses before this it speaks about a man named Jacob who killed his brother and was sent away by his father because his mother was concerned about his safety. In verses 15-17, on his journey after being sent away, he stopped in one place to rest. Laid down and started dreaming. This place he was resting in must have looked scary. Jacob feared in the place of which he was sent but, the Lord spoke to him by dream, to ease his mind. To let him know he would be safe wherever he went. He would guard him along his travels, and He wouldn't leave him.

Genesis 28:15-17 says, "I am with you and will keep you in all places that you go and will bring you again into this land; for I will not leave you, until I have done that which I have spoken to you. And Jacob awaked out of his sleep, and he said, Surely the Lord is in this place; and I knew it was not. And he was afraid, and said, how dreadful is this place! This none other but the house of God and this is the gate of heaven."

While reading these scriptures I clearly heard the Lord say for me to go to San Diego for 30 days and stay with an associate of mine, of whom I met when she came to visit Chicago. He said to stay no longer than 30 days. He said the place I was going to would look dreadful but, know the Lord was there with me. It would look scary, but the Lord was in this place.

I'm thinking, how am I going to stay with her, and she lives in a shelter. God surely couldn't possibly want me to sleep in a shelter. I kept hearing, "Go where she is". Of course, I obeyed what the Lord said. I loaded up my truck. My mom and I drove to San Diego. It was the scariest ride of our life. We prayed we would never have to take that drive ever in life again. I prayed in tongues so much during that drive. We thought about having someone fly to Colorado to help us, (which is where we decided we couldn't take that drive anymore). The hills, valleys and mountains were scary as ever. But I knew I had to face one of my fears which was driving in the mountains. We prayed some more and got back on the road.

The plan was for my mom to help me drive and when we arrived in San Diego, she had to leave me, go to the airport to head back home. She couldn't go into the land with me of which God was leading me to..

Genesis 12:1 says, "Take no kindred (relative) with you into the land that God will show you".

This is an instruction the Lord gave me. So, I had to obey. My mom did not want to leave me. But, because she trusted God, she obeyed. This was a journey the Lord was taking me on, alone.

CHAPTER 4
THE SAN DIEGO EXPERIENCE

It was late when we made it into San Diego, so we stayed at a hotel. Then my mom left the next morning. I checked out of the hotel and made my way to meet my associate at this shelter. I had no idea what I was in for going to this shelter. I'd never experienced being at a shelter. I knew the Lord gave me scripture to prepare me for this place, but to my eyes was I surprised.

I met with my associate at the shelter. Now, she had recently gotten approved to stay at a brand-new transitional housing facility. It was beautiful. I thought she was going to be staying at the other shelter with me. But I didn't find out she had been accepted in this new program until I arrived. There was a long list of which I would have to sign to get in the new building.

I drove to the shelter where I would be staying, with all my belongings in my truck. I remember thinking, God was going to work a miracle by moving me to California. I thought he was going to open the windows of heaven and many blessings were going to come my way. Like having a beautiful apartment or home so that I could send for my kids. I had no idea I was getting ready to have a serious EXPERIENCE. While driving toward the place I see people sleeping on the sidewalks, tents on the sidewalk, every walk of life you can name was on the streets. This was the downtown streets of San Diego. I could not understand how a beautiful city with so much wealth had so much poverty, especially downtown. I was like, "Oh my God". I said, "Jesus you have got to be kidding me". There were so many homeless people around. Drug addicts, young and old, men and women. I had never seen anything like this before. Here I am a Chicago girl. I saw drug addicts and homeless people back home, but never at this level. Surely God surprised me. Throughout my journey I remember thinking, there was no way in the world I could share this experience with my family or friends. They would surely think I lost my mind. I could hear them saying, "She gave all she had up to follow Jesus and live like this".

Matthew 19:29 it says, "And everyone that hath forsaken houses, or brethren, or sisters, or father, or mother, or wife, or children, or lands, for my sake, shall receive a hundredfold, and shall inherit everlasting life". I was living this scripture, for real.

I drove to the front of this place and it's a huge white tent that holds hundreds of people, both men and women. This place was called, "The Tent". They weren't too picky about who they allowed to stay there. I was glad God prepared me with scripture as to the description of this place before I came. This was a dreadful looking place from the outside because of the many people wandering around. I must say they kept it very clean and sanitary. It had to be because every walk of life was there. This tent had bunk beds for over 200 people. Men in the back and ladies in the front. They supplied food but I supplied my own. They had curfew so there was a certain time you had to be back in the tent, or you were locked out. They had showers on the outside, portable toilets and bowls to brush your teeth. I could not believe this was a part of my journey. But I was in it. I knew there was a plan and God was showing me some things. I just didn't know what He was showing me at the time. I was a little nervous about parking my truck on the street because I had so much stuff in it. But on street parking was the only parking available. The security advised me to get there early so I could park close to the entrance. God is so good. The security guards told me they would keep an eye on my truck if I could park close. So, every night I tried getting there early.

 I know all this sounds crazy. Many may say, "I wouldn't have lived like this". But this was my journey. This was a plan God had set aside for me.

 I remember a friend of mine telling me God could not allow me to experience homelessness in my own city. I know this to be true. My family and friends would have been a distraction and interference. I would not have been able to learn all the information I learned and experience what God wanted me to experience.

I stayed at the tent for only 4 to 5 days. The Lord granted me favor. He had a plan. I had applied for the new transitional housing building my associate was living in. I applied the 1st day I arrived in San Diego.

There was a waiting list so long to get in this new state of the art building. **"But, God is able to do exceedingly and abundantly above all we could ask or think", (Ephesians 3:20).** There were steps to getting into this building. I remember having to get a TB shot. I didn't have to get a shot to stay at The Tent. Their main concern was providing shelter for whoever. But at this transitional housing building, there were criteria's that had to be met. It was a much safer and secure environment.

Moving to this building was a breath of fresh air. I mentioned my associate was no longer staying in the tent but in this new transitional housing building. So, my 30 days of living with her had started when I moved there. Living there was quite an experience. There were young and old women in this program. This program was designed to help men and women get back to living a civilized life. It provided a stable roof over one's head while they focused on finding a job. They had their rules but because it was a new building and new program it was flexible. I guess because they were learning themselves.

I have been around so many dysfunctional people during this journey and I've learned there are a lot of people with mental issues. I sometimes feel I can be of counsel to mental patients, even though I have not attended a school for a degree but, my experiences have taught me how to deal with their emotions. Many of them were crazy and out of their mind. That's another level of mental and I believe God can heal them. Now, I'm not being mean when I use the word crazy. Through my years of experience from being around these types of people I notice they are not in their right mind. Many of the women in this facility, at some point in their life had been abused, beaten, on drugs, alcoholics, molested, lost a job, lost their home, raped and heartbroken. The issues of life can take a toll on one which caused a lot of these people to lose it all, which resulted in them being homeless and some out of their minds. Many of them didn't know how to deal with pain and suffering. So, some resulted in taking pills, like depression medication. They just couldn't figure out how to come out of the pit they were in.

That's why God sends his people, leaders, disciples into these dark places to reach and teach them that there is light on the other side. That Jesus (Yeshua) is the way. They just have to open their heart and mind and receive. Allow the spirit of the Lord in to open their eyes and direct them to a peaceful path. When being used as an instrument for God, sometimes you can reach many people at one time. And sometimes it's to be done one soul at a time. In my case, it was one soul at a time on this journey and experience.

I learned a lot from this program. They offered a lot to help people get back to life. You couldn't just sit around feeling sorry for yourself. You had to get up off your butt and find a solution. They offered many resources, such as, clothes for interviews, computer rooms, counselors etc.

At this point in my journey, I was still trying to figure out why the Lord would make me go through something like this. The associate of mine who I was living in this shelter with, was at a low point in her life. The Lord showed me, being there would help to uplift her. She needed some Holy Spirit and faith teaching around her. She needed light spoken into her. She was very ill at the time. I didn't know this when I first arrived in San Diego. I mean, it was a life or death situation for her. We would pray and pray and believe God for healing in her body. She was a fitness expert of many years but who would have thought her healthy body would take such a turn. It was a long process but in due time she was healed. To God be the glory.

CHAPTER 5
PEOPLE TEST YOU

My faith was tested so strongly in that transitional housing facility in San Diego. It was tested by a woman living there. There was an older lady who would pick on everybody in the place. She would cuss them out. She was mean. Guess who was her roommate? Yes, you guessed it, Me. She harassed everybody. I tried being quiet and staying out of her way. I would keep my headphones on often. I remember one time I was listening to music and started singing. She told me to shut up. It was so funny (As I think back to those moments, I laugh). Although she was mean, there were some really funny moments. I have a funny sense of humor. I love to laugh and make jokes out of everything. Especially in a dark moment. But I had reached a breaking point. I was at the end of my road. Meaning, I was ready to leave this place. I had enough of everything and everybody. I had been keeping peace around this little old lady. Some of the other ladies were telling me to report her to the staff. They knew I was tired of her picking with me. Our rooms had no doors on them, so you could hear and see everything going on in every room. They would often hear her harassing me. I'm not the type to snitch. I just try to ignore or eventually I will confront the individual. She picked with me every day. I would let her have her way. She cussed at me. I remember when she cussed the lady in the wheelchair. I felt so sorry for her. Then she came into the room yelling and snapping on me afterwards. The next thing to happen was I started talking back to her really loud. Telling her how mean she was to everybody. Telling her how ashamed she should be for a woman her age. I told her she has harassed me and everybody in here long enough. I said so much. I can't remember everything. But I spoke to that devil that was inside her picking on everybody. The spirit man stood up in me to go toe to toe with that evil spirit inside her. She was starting to feel embarrassed. She tried quieting me. She whispered, "Be quiet before we get in trouble". Loudly, I said, "Oh, now you want to be quiet". I got louder and said, "No, it's too late now. I don't care who hears me. The people in this building know I don't bother anyone, but you have really pushed my buttons". I never cussed at her. She was still an elder and I respect that. But God himself in heaven knew everybody had enough of her. I was concerned about being put out of the program, but we met with the advisers and they were very understanding. Because I finally stood up to her, she apologized. She turned so much nicer to me as time went on. I remember her coming in the room offering me cookies and all types of snacks. She loved sweets. She would sneak them in the room.

After we had that moment, she started opening up to me. She started sharing her childhood with me and what happened with her in past relationships. I guess she felt close to me now. She told me her reason for being in the shelter. She said she'd actually prefer sleeping on the streets because she didn't like people telling her what to do. I guess she needed a little break from sleeping on the concrete. She was so used to sleeping outside. I remember every night she slept with a bunch of clothes on. I asked her if she was afraid of being sexually assaulted or any harm being done to her by sleeping on the street. She said no, she felt safe out there. She said they were good to her. She had traveled on the bus a lot to different states. She had a check she would receive monthly. So, she survived off it. I remember her saying how she was getting too old to be sleeping on the streets. She was waiting for some money and approval for a small room she would rent in an apartment building. She was ready to leave the facility we were in because of their rules. I believe the love and kindness I showed her in the beginning made this little old lady overlook when I snapped on her. It opened her heart to receive what the Lord would have me to say to her in our time of communing. Even though the other women would cuss her out when she said something to them, I stayed kind to her. My snapping broke a chain between us. She knew I was kind, and she took it for granted. But I knew she felt bad knowing she'd pushed a button to anger me. Although I snapped, it was a loving reality check behind it. Which made her soften up and stop being so mean. She wanted to be my friend. She was sad when I told her I was leaving. Me and some of the other ladies were quite surprised to see this emotional side to her.

    I often think about her and wonder how she's doing. She captured a piece of my heart. Underneath all that toughness was a soft loving short, little old white-haired funny lady.

"Life situations can turn you into someone you are not supposed to be, if you allow it".

"Love is the greatest command. Love is patient, love is kind, it does not envy, it does not boast, it is not proud. It does not dishonor others, it is not self-seeking, it is not easily angered, it keeps no record of wrongs. Love does not delight in evil but rejoices with the truth. It always protects, always trusts, always hopes, always perseveres. Love never fails", (1Corinthians 13:4-8).

So, I started my California experience in San Diego with about $3,000. I didn't know what I was to do when it ran out. I didn't know where I was going or what I was doing. I only knew what to do when the Holy Spirit gave me instructions. I had a truck note, car insurance, cell bill, and food expenses. I had no knowledge of how long that money was to last. So, with my unknowing I had to still think smart about how I spent my money.

I tried to find a job doing hair at a salon in San Diego. I knew I only had 30 days there, but I was still trying to keep money in my pocket. I couldn't find work. It was like, I didn't fit out there. And of course, I didn't because I wasn't going to stay in San Diego.
I heard my next instruction from the Lord which was to go to LA. So, I left the facility in San Diego. My associate was sad I was leaving. I was sad to leave her, but I knew I had to keep moving. She wanted

to come along. The Holy Spirit had already told me she would want to come but, I was to drive to LA alone.

In the book of Genesis Chapter 12 verse 1 it says, "Now the Lord had said unto Abram, get thee out of thy country, and from thy father's house, unto a land that I will show thee".

The Lord put that scripture back in my remembrance because my heart is so soft. I feel sorry for people and want to help everybody. I want to take everybody with me through this faith walking experience. But I had to remember the Lord was taking me on a journey at this time. What little did I know is everybody would still be allowed to go on this experience of faith with me, as they read my books.

CHAPTER 6
THE DREAM CENTER EXPERIENCE

What I am about to share with you happened maybe one year before my trip to San Diego and my California experience of homelessness started. There is a place called, "The Dream Center" in LA. I was a part of their program one year before I went on this California experience. They have a program called "Discipleship". I remember sitting at home one day watching tv and hearing about all the good this ministry was involved in with the community. So, I sowed $1,000 into this program through Pastor Jentezen Franklin (I had money at this point of my life). He is an awesome preacher and was a spokesman for the Dream Center, at that time.

I remember hearing in my spirit I would be a $1,000 seed sower. And I still believe today. I believe in sowing and reaping and helping those in need.

The Dream Center touched my heart. I love how they help many broken people and give them a place of refuge. They give to the community and help the poor. So, I remember wanting to be a part of what they were contributing to society. But I desired full insight. I thought I would intern with them to see how their program worked. What little did I know was I was going to be a living being in this program. The Discipleship Program was set up for people looking for refuge. People could stay for one year. It was for men and women who are overcoming life-controlling issues and overcoming drug and alcohol addiction, depression and abuse. This program is structured to eliminate distractions so that participants can focus on building a healthy foundation to rebuild their lives. They provide physical, spiritual and emotional care, food, housing, education and counseling. Free of charge. There were people from all across the map, different race, sex, no discrimination.

I was in prayer one day and I clearly heard the Lord say, "You are going in the discipleship program as if you are one of them". As I stated, there was a pull inside of me that wanted to see how this program operated. This wasn't a program I could just read about. I needed hands on, visual, total insight. Honestly, I would have preferred to pay and intern but that was not the God Plan. It was like the Lord was telling me intern was the easy way and I wouldn't get to see the hidden things of the program unless I was one of the women in the program. I remember crying and thinking oh my God, I can't leave my kids for a year. Although I wasn't sure how long the Lord would have me in this program. Besides, I felt I would stick out like a sore thumb. I knew for sure they would know I hadn't come from a broken home or suffered any abuse. Especially not from a level of where they were in life.

I remember asking the Lord, what reason would I give them for entering this program and the Holy Spirit gave it to me. I shared with them the word hardship and how I was losing my home and how I wasn't working at the time. I really believe this was all God's doing, getting me into this program. Because unto this day I still don't know how using the word hardship got me into that program. But God had a plan. There was an interview over the phone. They accepted me. I knew this was the favor of God. Besides, my spirit had already let me know this was the direction I was supposed to go in.

Although this was a one-year program. I'm grateful the Lord allowed me to only stay 7 days. I learned so much in so little time. I learned the daily operation of this program. You know how you go to school to learn or how you take a couple of classes or even when you attend a conference for one week? This is how the Lord used me with the Dream Center. I went to school for about one week to learn and see one on one how to run a discipleship program. I call it the school of hard knocks. I know God has a plan for me to use everything I learned from this program.

I also learned God will send you from one side of the map to the other side of the map to help and encourage another soul. This happened while in the program as well. I connected with two women in the program. One was married and she shared with me her issue was she drank alcohol a lot. The other was a lesbian. She was raped when she was young by a couple of men. So, this turned her heart and so she desired to be with women. I won't use names, but these are all true stories. The one who was an alcoholic cried all day for the first two days of entering the program. She didn't want to get out of bed. The staff didn't force her. I remember praying silently by my desk in our room for her. There were about 8 to 10 women in a room. She would cry and cry and cry. When we first came into the program the staff weren't pushy at all because they knew how hard it was for everyone to leave their families. If I can remember, we weren't allowed to talk to our family in the beginning. I remember when I told my mom and kids, they wouldn't hear from me for a while. They were very disturbed by this. But this was one of the steps in this program. It's all part of the healing, discipline and disconnection that had to happen in order to get people committed to the program. Remember, many of these people in this program were not disciplined, had no order in their lives, or spiritual guidance. But this was a program formed by believers, people who believed in discipleship. So, my family and I had to look past all the rules I had to follow because I knew God sent me there for purpose.

When the married lady started opening up to me, she mentioned she voluntarily came into this program. Her husband loved her dearly, she had children but, she knew she needed help and her husband wanted her to get help as well. I remember one night at bedtime she was crying. Everyone was in bed. We had to be in our bunks by a certain time. Everything was done like clockwork. Our bunks were next to each other. I whispered her name. I slept with my prayer shawl over me every night. That was my point of contact that I used as my covering. I told her to come over and sit with me. I remember us sitting on my bed. I put my prayer shawl over her and my head. I asked her if she believed in praying in tongues. She responded yes. I let her know I would be praying over her in tongues. So, I proceeded. I don't know how long I prayed. I finished, she got up and went back to bed. The next morning, she got out her bed, came to shower time, got dressed and she joined the rest of us in our classes. When I tell you, the power of prayer in the Holy Spirit can heal a broken heart, she was a living example. Because for the first two days she did not want to get out of bed. But the Holy Spirit is so real. She started talking and communicating with others. I found out she had a relationship with God. She told me she was very familiar with praying in tongues. She was just in a dark place. She called me her friend. I pray to this day she is doing much better.

The other young lady I became cool with was a lesbian who was raped a few times. She was kind of cold hearted when we met. Like stand-offish. Not only toward me but to others. She had to play this hard-core woman. But the Lord allowed me to see right through her. On my desk I had pictures of my family and a bible. She would often walk pass my desk but say nothing. Then one day she says, "Why are you here". She said it in a nice, friendly way. In my head I am laughing and thinking, "Oh I'm caught". She said, "There is nothing wrong with you". I shared with her how the Lord sent me there. I started sharing with her my relationship with God. She already knew I was a spiritual woman; she would often see me reading my bible. We started talking more often. I remember her asking why God would allow the rape to happen to her. She was very hurt by that. She looked to me as a big sister in such a short period of time. I remember her telling me the Lord sent me there for her. I told her I believe that and know that to be true. I'd hope her being in that program would help to bring healing to her soul as well.

At first, I thought I was there to learn about the discipleship program. But when I met these two ladies, I knew there was much more to my experience there. We hung out in the garden. The Dream Center had a garden, and we would all go as a group. It was a time of meditation. The lesbian girl was kind of rebellious with others but for some reason she had a level of respect for me. I loved her like a little sister. She told me what happened in her childhood, which caused her to live the way she was living. We talked about a lot of things. I shared some things about myself and family with her. She sat under me like a little sister who was being protected. She was much younger than me.

When it was time to leave the program, I felt so sad and bad because I was leaving them both. The one who was the lesbian told me she knew I was going to leave way before the year ended. She cried and I felt so bad. I kind of wanted to stay for the sake of her because I felt like I could help her more. She was starting to open up with the other ladies as well. When I told her, I was leaving I noticed how she started changing a little with the other women. It was as if she was shutting down again. Being stand-offish again. I knew she was just a little angry because I was leaving.

I started missing my family by the fifth day. Then I started itching. They didn't have bed bugs or anything. It was my nerves. That's how I knew this journey was coming to an end. Even though it was a one-year program, they allowed you to leave whenever you were ready. They wanted you to stay but they would not force you. By the 6th day I clearly heard my go from the Lord. I was being released from this assignment. I met with the young lady of whom I looked to as a little sister on the 7th day, to give my goodbye. She gave me a big hug and her favorite sunglasses (which she always hid behind). I called my mom and told her I am coming home. She was so surprised I was coming back so early. I wanted to surprise my children, so she kept it a secret. I remember when I returned home, I cried like a baby. Because I missed the girls from the Dream Center. I felt like I let them down by not staying longer. That brought such pain to my heart, but I knew I'd served my purpose for being there.

PRAYER

I hope and pray this book finds its way to that young lady I met at the Dream Center. I pray her heart has been healed and made whole, in the mighty name of Jesus (Yeshua), Amen.

CHAPTER 7
THE LA EXPERIENCE

I was truly being led by the Holy Spirit. I often fast and prayed during this journey. Fasting kept me in tune with the voice of the Lord. I could hear clearly. Whether it was from reading the word of God, during my prayer time, visual, listening to a gospel teaching or watching something on tv. I was able to identify when the Lord was speaking to me. Fasting kept me from making wrong decisions. In my last book I spoke about how often I fast, the number of days and how quickly I would receive an answer from the Lord. During the life journey and experience in California I had to do the same thing.

I remember arriving in LA and saying, "Ok Lord I am here where should I stay". I heard nothing about getting a hotel room because as I mentioned, I only had so little money left to spend. So, I was trying to be a good steward over what I had left. But I clearly heard in my spirit to go to the Dream Center.

After leaving San Diego, I parked in the Dream Center Parking lot hoping I could go into the facility and have a place to stay. I went inside to speak with someone about housing. That didn't work out for me. I should have known that was not a part of God's plan. I heard in my spirit to go there but that didn't necessarily mean I would be sleeping inside.

It turned dark and I am praying, "Lord, I have no place to go. You have not told me where to sleep". This journey was all about being Spirit led every step of the way. Not trying to figure it out for myself but quieting myself to hear from God. Then the thought came to mind of me sleeping in my truck. I thought back on how the Lord made it possible for me to bring my truck with me to California. It was a must that I kept my truck. I honestly did not want to keep it. I was willing to start all over in California, a new land, meet new people and have new things. When I was home in Chicago, I tried giving the truck back to the dealership because I knew I was leaving for California. They did not want it and I did not want to drive to California. Shipping the truck was not an option. So, with all that going on, I knew the Lord had a different plan then mine. I just didn't know what. So, I kept the truck.

While sitting in my truck parked in the parking lot of the Dream Center, it clicked in my head, "Oh my God I'm going to be sleeping in here". It was like a delayed reaction. I'm thinking, "Lord you have got to be kidding me. Have mercy on me". I thought, "Why am I sleeping in my truck". All that time I had no idea the plan would be for me to sleep in my truck. But I was so into this journey and being led by the Spirit of God that I couldn't care. I stood firm on the words, "Hear and Obey". No matter what it looked like I had to hear and obey. I remember hiding so people couldn't see me at night because I didn't want to get put out of the parking lot. During the day I would find something to do. Like go to the park. There was one beautiful park near the Dream Center. But there were homeless people everywhere. I couldn't believe my eyes. I saw so many women on the street as well. I was so disturbed by this. One night while sleeping in my truck, my heart was so heavy thinking about the young women who were sleeping on the streets. I knew it was not safe. I would cry and pray for them. **The bible says, "Call for the mourning women, let them take up a wailing", (scripture Jeremiah 9:17,18).** That was definitely what I was doing. I was so grateful to have a vehicle to sleep in. These women had a cold concrete. Their safety was an issue, so I cried loud to God and spared not for their safety.

   I was at the park one day holding a conversation with this old man. He asked where I was from. It was the daytime. I normally would leave that park by the late evening. I believe he saw me a couple times at the park. I often went there to wash my face, hands and brush my teeth. I had found a facility to take showers. Being out on the streets I washed my hands every 10 minutes it seemed. Anyway, the old man pulled a stack of bills out his pocket. And then he says, "I know I look homeless, but I have some money". I just looked at him and said, "Good for you". Then he says, "Let me know if I can help you and be careful at night. I have the keys to the gate if you need to get in". When I left the park, I thought about what he said. Then I thought, "Hold up did this man just try to proposition me for sex". It hadn't dawned on me at first. I thought, the nerve of him. I realized this is probably what happens to a lot of women on the streets.

When I went back to the park, I would see him. He would wave, I waved but never talked to him again. I didn't want no trouble and I hoped he didn't either. I knew God had me safe in his arms. But God gave me wisdom as well. So, I stayed far away from him.

Sometimes that devil will tell you exactly what he wants. We just have to listen when people are talking. Have an ear to hear exactly what they are saying. In this case the man said for me to be careful at night. Which meant he was probably up to no good at night. Therefore, I needed to take heed to those words and be nowhere around.

With that man trying to proposition me, I felt a little sadness because the Lord showed me that in desperate situations, this is what some women are subjected to, in need to survive. They are in desperate need of money and so they have sex in exchange. Then one trick turns into numerous tricks to survive on the streets.

The streets of LA were dark and scary. I was taken by a total surprise. I saw all types of things while out there especially at night. There is an old song called, "The freaks come out at night". I saw a whole lot of weird freaky things. It was scary and distasteful. When I was out at night, I had to keep a don't mess with me look on my face. I had to discern when, who and what was safe. It was a party for many at night but not for me. I had to be on guard and pray. I had to stay in the spirit, pray, read my bible often as ever and I would always listen to my Pastor Bill Winston on Wednesday and Sundays, no matter what part of California I was living. This was an instruction from God as well. I was now to be under his teachings for the journey and season I was in. Every teaching he taught led me into my next step. I stayed in LA, the Dream Center parking lot for about 5 days. Then the Lord brought to my remembrance a conversation I had on the phone with an old childhood friend when I was in San Diego. Before that conversation I hadn't talked to him in years. We talked on the phone a few times while I was in San Diego. He lived in California. Unknowingly, God had already mapped out a plan for me on my journey. We were having casual conversations and catching up on lost years. Sharing our accomplishments in life, downfalls and what we wanted to accomplish in our future.

One night while sitting in my truck I said, "Lord I am cold and tired of moving around in this truck". Temperatures drop tremendously at night in California. It's the kind of cold that freezes your bones. I slept in so many positions trying to get comfortable. The Lord told me to call that childhood friend and let him know I have been sleeping in my truck for 5 days. I was like, "Lord that is embarrassing". I was glad I was away from home in this experience because it would have been embarrassing and shameful. I knew the average person would not understand why I would be living this way. After, being in this homeless experience for so long I no longer cared what anybody thought. I had to survive and make it through this spiritual journey and experience. I knew there was a purpose behind it. I had my mom and my only spiritual friend (at the time) as my support team. I confided in my spiritual friend about the Lord telling me to call that childhood friend and to let him know I had been sleeping in my truck for 5 days. She gave me a good spiritual get over the embarrassment talk. It's about surviving. She said, "You know this could be a test for him as well". Which is true. I've learned God likes to see where the heart of his people lay. Will they have compassion or don't care. Well, I worked up the nerve to call him because I couldn't take sleeping another night in my truck.

    I told him and he said I could come stay there for a few days because he would be leaving town for an extended period. His work required him to travel. I said, "Ok".

CHAPTER 8
JUST A LITTLE REST IN ENCINO

I arrived at my childhood friend's place. I was so happy I didn't know what to do. I had a couch to sleep on and I was so excited. He actually understood my situation and understood the sacrifice. Because I was definitely sacrificing my way of living for this experience God was giving me. I shared with him how I'm being led by the Holy Spirit by coming to California. He asked about my plans. All I knew was, I wanted to live in Pasadena California. He was really cool about everything I shared with him. He never treated me like the circumstance I was living.

During this journey I always kept myself up to par. Hair styled, clothes up to par, clean truck and an up to date phone. Believe it or not people looked at all this during my journey. Looking up to par helped me a lot. It got me into certain places and around certain people and favor from them. You would be amazed at how people judge you by your appearance. You could be financially broke as ever and people do not know it when you are keeping yourself up to code with material things. That's just the world we live in. So, I have learned you have to play the game. It worked for me on this journey. The Lord already told me in the beginning of my journey that men would help me. So, with that being said I knew I had to keep a great appearance. Besides, most people living in LA know it's a struggle to get established there. We always hear stories from celebrities of their struggle and how some had to sleep in their car to survive until they made it. Which means they experienced homelessness. It's not everybody's story but, many people I spoke with had a struggle moving to LA, going after their dreams and purpose. I did not want that for myself but at this point in my journey, I didn't know what to expect to make it in California. Many people I came in contact with along the way were cool. They knew me as the Chicago girl who was trying to survive and make it in California. I allowed many to think this. I couldn't tell everyone I was on a spiritual journey. They wouldn't understand that. It's hard explaining spirit to unspirited minded people. So, I rolled with their opinion. Well, at least that's what I allowed them to think.

I couldn't look at this experience as a struggle. Even though sometimes it felt that way. God was doing something different within me and as a believer I had to remember I'm in the world but not of the world.

1 John 4:5,6 says, "They are from the world; therefore, they speak from the world's viewpoint; and the world listens to them. We are from God. Whoever knows God listens to us; whoever is not from God doesn't listen to us. This is how we distinguish the Spirit of truth from the spirit of error".

John 17:14-16 says, "I have given them your word, and the world hated them, because they do not belong to the world-just as I myself do not belong to the world. I don't ask you to take

them out of the world, but to protect them from the evil one. They do not belong to the world, just as I do not belong to the world".**

My childhood friend I was staying with at the time, explained to me he would be leaving town for weeks, for work and had already told a friend of his they could hang out at his place while he was gone. So, he was giving me the heads up that I would have to leave. I'm like Lord I am not physically or mentally ready to go back in the streets. But God always has a plan mapped out. **He is the alpha and omega, the beginning and the end, (Revelation 1:8).** God knows everything. I was put in a position where I had to trust God. This entire journey was about experience and trusting God. So, if it was time to go back into the streets, I had to go. But I prayed, my spiritual friend back home prayed, and my mom prayed. Of course, my mom was a nervous wreck. Knowing her daughter was sleeping in a car bothered her. But all her trust was in God.

I said, "Ok" to my childhood friend when he told me the plan. But I was silently thinking, for him to tell his friend he can't come. I felt I had a dire need. I didn't want to interfere with God's plan with me, so I didn't say what I was thinking out loud. I knew I was sent out here on purpose. I was still unsure at this point why, but I was there. So, I had to allow God's plan to play out.

Then, the next day my friend says to me, "Change of plans, you can stay". I believe I took the deepest breath, because I was so relieved. The Lord worked that thing out. I was happy. I believe my childhood friend knew I would take better care of his place than his friend. Because he would be gone for almost 30 days. God will move things and people around for us.

    I must say, I am so grateful that he trusted me. He hadn't seen me in so many years. We were kids when I last saw him. He says he saw me at a salon I worked at back in Chicago, but I didn't see him. It was a divine connection from God. It was all a part of God's plan.

I spent much of my time getting to know the city I was spending 30 days in and getting much rest. I enjoyed walking through parks pulling lemons from trees. I could not believe I had access to so many lemon trees. I experienced working out in the park. They actually had workout machines outdoors. This was all new to me and I was so amazed. Being in this city for 30 days gave me a wonderful experience of what California offered. I believe this time of rest was preparing me (unknowingly) for what God had ahead of me.

Many back home may have thought I was in California living it up when I first moved out there. That was not the case. Waking up every day to the sun and beautiful palm trees was wonderful. But some of the things I journeyed through were not fun. All pride and humiliation had to be put to the side. It was truly an **EXPERIENCE**.

    Time passed and it was getting closer to my childhood friend's return home. I knew it would be time for me to exit. I was not to be a burden on him. He didn't ask where I was going, I was so glad he didn't because I didn't know where I was going, and I didn't want him to think I needed sympathy. I was on a journey and I knew it. But I was on an unknown journey full of experiences. It was an assignment by God. So, I had to continue to be led by the Holy One.

"Stand strong in the Lord and in the power of His might", Ephesians 6:10.

I am forever grateful for my childhood friend being there when I needed him most. If you are reading this you know who you are, Thank you.

We must always keep ourselves available to be used by God. Keep a heart of love.

CHAPTER 9
THE INGLEWOOD EXPERIENCE

My money was getting lower. I was sitting in my truck and went into a time of prayer. I said, "Lord where do you want me to go next". I heard the word, "Inglewood". I said, "Sweet Jesus, Inglewood". As I'm typing this now, I am laughing, and thinking was God mad at me that he wanted to send me to Inglewood. When I think of Inglewood, I think of Ice Cube, Snoop Dogg, and more of the west coast rappers and how they rapped about guns, sex and violence, everything came to my mind. I couldn't see this being a place of peace like Encino and Pasadena California.

The Lord sent me to a specific church out there. So, I left my childhood friend's parking lot and drove to Inglewood.

I drove into the parking lot of the church. I'd listened to many of this Pastor's teachings. He is what I like to call one of the Generals of faith. I listened to his entire series on Faith before coming to California, not knowing I would visit that church one day. I did attend one of their Sunday services while I was staying at my childhood friend's place. I couldn't wait to go see how they could help me find somewhere to live.

I can now laugh at this experience because at this part of my journey in Inglewood, I really thought I was going to find a place to live and I was going to use my faith to get it. One would call this type of faith, "Presumption Faith".

I know all this sounds so crazy up to this point. But this was my journey and my experience that I allowed faith to take me on.

I made the mistake of not listening to the Holy Spirit. Since the church was closed, I went driving around, like a tourist. I now laugh at this experience as well. I was driving down a main street in Inglewood. I saw a mattress laid straight up on a fence, cats crawling all on it, many homeless people on the sidewalk, chairs, tore up sofas, drug addicts, prostitutes, you name it, I saw it. That's not the funny part. The funny part was how fast I drove right back to the parking lot of the church. I remember feeling like I drove out of safety to what looked like a jungle with lions, tigers and bears. I thought, I'd better get my butt back to safety before something happens. I had a holy fear of the Lord to come upon me that let me know I could be in danger.

Sometimes we don't know what God is protecting us from. God is a keeper.

Psalm 121:5 KJV says, "The Lord is thy keeper: The Lord is thy shade on your right hand".

There is a song I love called, "Perfect Peace" by Earnest Pugh. There is a line in the song that says, "He is the keeper of my soul". God is the keeper of our soul. He took really good care of me through this journey. He can and will keep you. No matter what your situation may be. God will keep you.

So, I'm at the church. I believe it was the weekend and the business office of the church was closed. I remember sitting in my truck parked thinking, "Oh my God what am I to do". There was no security in the lot when I arrived. So, once again I slept in my truck.

The next morning someone tapped on my window and asked can they help me. I explained to them I moved here from Chicago and I'm here to get some help to find a place to live. He was kind of clueless as to the help I could receive. But he suggested I speak with someone in the church office. He told me what time and day they would be open. It seems there was some type of event going on for the weekend. He said I couldn't sleep in the lot for security and safety purposes. I can tell he didn't want to put me out since it was daytime, so he then told me I could park in a different area of the parking lot, closer to his security box. But by the evening I would have to leave, and he'd hope I would get help from the church.

So, I drove toward the downtown area that night. I had driven around Inglewood during the daytime. Looking in different areas, familiarizing myself with the streets. I found a cozy spot in the downtown area, near a planet fitness center. This is where I'd planned to park and sleep. I used a gym called planet fitness to workout, shower, comb my hair and whatever other maintenance I needed. By this time, I figured out, I was on a journey where I was experiencing homelessness. Something I really didn't sign up for with the Lord. At least, that's what I thought but, the Lord was preparing me for something.

The day approached for me to go speak with someone at the church for help, I was prepared and ready. Now, I didn't look broke down, like I needed help. All I had was my word, my story, my faith and God. The hour came. I went inside the church to meet with a lady. We spoke, I explained my situation and she said she was so sorry because they couldn't help me. She said the church didn't have anything set up to help people in transition or that was in my condition. She looked so sad and disappointed as she came out of the office to tell me this bad news. Then she hands me a list of city shelters she printed herself. Then says, "You don't look like you should go to any of these". She said I felt bad bringing this list to you. She explained to me the type of people that are at these shelters.

These shelters were the lowest, to my understanding. She knew it would be a dangerous place for me. I knew I had a better chance at safety by sleeping in my truck. I'm not knocking this church but, I must admit I was very disappointed in them. I feel the church should be a place that people should be able to go for help. I would much rather she said they have a program set up to help and house women but, it is full right now or had some type of temporary solution like some of the other churches did, as I will share with you later in this book. My spirit would have taken that rejection better. I do pray after the conversation I had with the nice lady, that changes were made to accommodate women in need. I gave her a strong word from the Lord to better how they should help those in need. She stood in agreement with the message, received it and thanked me.

During my journey the Lord showed me how many churches and ministries have no help for people who are looking for transitional housing. Transitional Housing can be used for people who are in an in between stage of life. They may have lost their home, job, going through a divorce, domestic violence etc. There are lots of recovery homes for drug addicts. But there is a need for more programs dealing with transitional housing.

Well, I walked out of that church feeling some type of way. And not a good way. The security guard stopped me and asked if they could help me. I said not at all. I showed him the list of shelters. With a concerned look on his face he said, "No, you can't go there". I already knew it was not part of the plan for me to sleep in those shelters in Inglewood.

Before I spoke with the lady at the church I slept in Inglewood for a couple of days. I believe it was the weekend and that's why their office was closed. I mentioned how I found a side street that looked safe in the downtown part of Inglewood. This was a much nicer area. As stated previously, I used the planet fitness facility to take showers and do my hair along with working out. I would keep my truck organized. I had some of my clothes on hangers because I didn't have an iron. I was glad my truck had tint on the windows, so no one could see inside. All shame and humility were gone out the window at this point.

During my experience in Inglewood I was looking at apartments to rent. I was hoping God would open a door for me. I was walking in faith, fasting and praying for favor. I looked at maybe 2 or 3 apartments. Remember, I had no money for a deposit for these apartments, no job but I was looking for a salon to work. Finding a salon out there was not hard. I worked at a salon for 1 day, which was on a Saturday. I was blessed to do a walk-in client. The salon was closed Sunday. I had time to sit and think. I realized that was not where I was supposed to stay for work. At the time I still didn't know Inglewood was not my final destination. But I knew I was running low on cash. I needed some money, so I had to do something. God already had a plan. I just needed to continue to hear and obey. The money I earned for that one day helped tremendously.

While looking for apartments I met a man who managed one of the buildings. While we were walking through the apartment we got on the topic of faith. I told him how the Holy Spirit led me to California. How I gave everything up to go on this journey, this walk of faith. He shared with me why he stopped going to church. He believed in God but just didn't like what was going on in the churches. He said he was a good person, and he was a giver but didn't want to be involved with the church stuff. I'm sure that's why many people have stopped attending church. Of course, I still spoke the love of God and truth into him.

He knew about my living situation and he asked what I was going to do since I was unable to get the apartment. I told him how I went to the church for help and they couldn't help me. He seemed really concerned. For some reason I shared every step I made with him. All the way up to me being present standing before him. I told him I would go back to the church and park in their parking lot until something comes to mind. He had my phone number because it was on file with the management company. I remember him looking at me as if he was trying to read me. He didn't know if I was lying or telling the truth because there were so many homeless people, scams, frauds in California and you couldn't trust anybody. I later found out; he was trying to decide if he should help me in some way.

I'm sitting in my truck. I don't remember if I was on the phone or listening to a gospel teaching. I always kept some gospel on because I needed more of the spirit of God, than flesh in my ear during this journey. My phone rings and it's the guy at the management company. He says, "Hey Fatima". He stated who he was and then said, "Your story checked out". I'm thinking, "What is he talking about". He checked behind every stop I made of which I shared with him being in Inglewood. From meeting with the lady at the church, he talked to the previous property manager I spoke with before I met him. I had given the previous property manager the same story (my truth). I figured what did I have to lose? Maybe someone would care and give me an apartment. He even spoke with the security guard at the church. He asked him if there was a lady in a black truck from Illinois in the parking lot. Remember, the security guard told me whenever I come in that lot to park near his security box. So, the security guard let him know I was parked there.

That's why it's good to be honest. A lie is hard to keep track of. You never know how help can come your way by telling the truth. I didn't know the man was going to help me. He said, "I'm going to pay to get you a room for the night". He told me he would drive and meet me at that church parking lot.

I think it's wonderful how people keep the heart of love to help, even when they're disappointed with the church. He didn't categorize me with the church but as an individual on her own spiritual journey with God. It disappointed him that the church could not help me.

He came and we sat in my truck and talked. He said, "I was looking at you and you didn't look like you needed help. His exact words were, "You look up to par and you have an up to date cell phone". Then we started laughing. I told him well thank God for that because this walk of faith is not easy. He then says, "Your stories checked out and I wanted to help you on this journey".

I'm sure most women would have been afraid to deal with a strange man, not knowing his motives. But I was not afraid. I prayed and trusted God that no evil shall come near my dwelling, (Psalm 91).

He found a motel for me to stay. This motel was up the street from where I saw the mattress, cats, lions, tigers and bears (a little exaggeration). It was dark looking from the outside but clean on the inside. So, I was thankful. He gets the room for me and says, "Would you like me to stay" (jokingly but serious). I look over to the right of me and I see a lamp. I'm thinking, if he makes one wrong move, I'm knocking him straight out. I politely said, "No, I should be fine, thank you". He says, "Are you sure" (with a little smirk on his face, of which he knew he didn't have a chance). I looked at him, and in a very stern and don't mess with me tone I said, "Yes". Then I remember saying, "Aren't you married anyway". He said he and his wife had an open relationship. I said, "That's not good but, ok and thank you for the room". I didn't want to start a discussion about his marriage. It was late. I was tired. My meeting with him served its purpose. So, he finally left. I am thankful for him as well.

I was able to get a good night's sleep. I woke up the next morning feeling so much better. My mind and body were rested probably because I had a bed to sleep in and not my truck. So, I leave the motel and park in front of the church. I remember clearly saying, "Ok Lord, where should I go next". I clearly heard, "Redondo Beach". I smiled when I heard Redondo Beach. I had been there before with my mom. An associate of hers moved from

Chicago to Redondo Beach and we visited her. Redondo Beach was surrounded by water, a place of refreshing. I absolutely love the water. It's very relaxing. I always saw myself living off the beach. Even in Chicago. Waking up every morning to that view and jogging along the beach. I'm thinking wow, maybe the Lord is going to open a door for me in Redondo. Still not knowing I was living, a homeless experience. At this point I still didn't know my final destination.

CHAPTER 10
THE RONDONDO BEACH EXPERIENCE

"You have arrived", says my GPS. It's so beautiful. The first place I drive to is the beach. I spent about 25 days in Redondo Beach. In the beginning, I didn't mind sleeping in my truck in Redondo Beach because it was so beautiful. I would always park near the beach so I could hear the water and so I could go walking at any time of the night. I felt so safe out there. The people were friendly. There were no street walkers. There were only a few homeless people that I saw, and they were polite.

I always kept an imagination. Never forgetting what I had before this homeless experience. Never forgetting the life, I lived. My homes, business, my children back home, mom, family and friends.

Thanks to my mom I was able to fly back home every so often, but only for a few days, never longer than a week or two. It's funny, how I would have to fly back to California to be homeless. Who does that? (Lol). Me, your Faith Sister. But this was the journey and experience the Lord gave me. My mom and my kids hated when it was time for me to go back. I, on the other hand, had mixed feelings. I didn't want to sleep in my truck but, I was also enjoying this moment to moment time I spent with God. This hearing and obeying moment. This shameful but very humbling experience.

During my journey I never told my kids I was sleeping in my truck. The only people who knew were my mom and my only spiritual friend I had at the time. My spiritual friend and I had started this walk of faith together. She was going through some experiences herself. We prayed for each other through our journey. The Lord connected us together. I mentioned in my last book how when I decided to take this walk of faith with God, I really didn't hang out with a lot of my friends anymore. They were in my life, but we just weren't around each other often. I was trying to get an understanding of what I was going through and I'm sure they didn't understand what I was going through as well. I'm sure many thought I was out of mind. But they never said it to me.

Besides no one in my circle of friends had ever mentioned anything about hearing from God or living a life of faith. Sure, many of us accepted Christ as our Lord and Savior and attended church on Sundays. But we never sat around each other making God the topic of the day. Then one day the Lord sends a new client my way. We became very close. She shared her thoughts with me, and I shared my thoughts with her. We saw we were pretty much thinking on the same level. The best part about this relationship is we were able to talk about God all the time. I hadn't had a friend I could do that with. Many of the people surrounding me didn't like her. I think they didn't like how a new person came into my life and we clicked. But it was the spirit of the living God inside of us that brought us together. She was quite bold, very open minded and opinionated. Most of the people didn't like that about her. But she was very informative. When she spoke, the room shook. Meaning, either you listened to her or you got mad at her. And, boy did some folks get mad at her. The ones that listened secretly, took heed to her words. I would laugh but keep quiet when she talked. I knew it served, it's purpose. Somebody needed to hear the information she would share. She had life experiences. I didn't care how people felt about her, I didn't let it stop us from having the relationship God was forming.

Anyway, after staying in beautiful Redondo Beach for about two weeks, I remember feeling tired and sore from sleeping in my truck. I was tired of the night chill, tired of trying to find the right position to sleep. I had body aches from sleeping in the wrong position. I remember going to the hospital. The doctor ran every test and found nothing wrong. I cried, "Lord I can't take this anymore".

I would meet with realtors to look at apartments and townhomes off the beach. These were million-dollar homes. One time a realtor told me where the keys were to the townhome. He gave me permission to enter the home alone. He said to lock up when I finished. I was surprised to hear the trust. So, I went inside, and it was so beautiful. Again, I had been praying to God for a beautiful place to live. I really wanted that townhome. I had no money, but I had great faith. I believed God could do anything. I also have learned through my experiences that if it's not His will for my life, it won't happen, or it may not be the time for it to happen.

There was beautiful furniture in every room. I said, "Lord this is living". I remember laying on the bed and not wanting to get up. I must admit, I thought about sleeping there. Then I woke up from that dream (lol). I didn't want to get myself arrested in this life experience.

I called my mom and told her how beautiful the place was. My mom is my biggest cheerleader. Whatever I did she was all for it. She believed in what I was hearing from God and the Lord would always put a confirmation in her spirit.

I left that townhome after staying there for about 30 minutes. I cried and cried. I still didn't understand why I was living the experience as a homeless person.

Somewhere during this part of my journey, I remember I was starting to lose sight of things. Then that spiritual friend of mine back home sent me a teaching by TD Jakes. He was teaching about getting lost in the journey. It was what I needed at that time. I just didn't know I was being taken on a journey to experience homelessness. The Holy Spirit did not reveal that to me in the beginning of this journey. I knew to hear and obey. I didn't know how long the money I came with on this journey would last. I didn't know what to do when it ran out. I didn't know I wasn't supposed to look for an apartment to live in LA, Inglewood or Redondo Beach. I hadn't realized this was a learning experience for me.

I was driving and saw a church. I told myself I would visit there on a Sunday. I fixed myself up well. Got my appearance together because I was determined to have the Pastor of that church help me. I was not taking no for an answer. It was a nice small congregation. The fellowship was good, but I was focused on getting help with a place to live. Then the Pastor taught a teaching on, "Disturbing God's Destiny". My heart dropped. I could have just passed out in my chair. I realized this is what I was getting ready to do. I would have interfered with God's plan because of what I wanted to do. Because I got in my feelings about this journey. I remember sitting there in that service quietly apologizing to God. I decided to shut my mouth, enjoy the service and part ways. Before church service started there was this lady with kids who was talking to me. She was very nice. But I remember I didn't want to do much chatting. I wanted to sit close enough to the front, so I could meet the Pastor. She was sitting towards the back and she wanted me to sit with her and her kids. I didn't want to sit next to her with all her kids. I know that sounds mean but I had my reason. I didn't want to be distracted because in my head I was on a mission and I didn't want anyone to interfere.

Well, service ended and this same lady with the kids walked up to me and asked how I liked the service. I told her I really enjoyed it. She then invited me to come downstairs to their fellowship hall. They were serving food and drinks. I'm thinking, "Great free food". That would save me some money. My funds were low.

I sat at a table with a few people. This little old lady starts talking to me. She asked where I was from and where I was sleeping. I told her where I was from but was hesitant about telling her where I was sleeping. I had just gotten a message from the Preacher and I did not want to disturb God's destiny in my life. I put my mind back in that place of being led by the Spirit of God. I wanted to see how God moved without me stepping in. I wanted to use my discernment. So, she asked me where I was sleeping again. I hesitantly and slowly was getting ready to tell her. But then she blurts out, "In your car. You're sleeping in your car, aren't you"? She said it so loudly. I was a little embarrassed. I don't like when people talk loudly. Especially, when you are right in front of their face. I also didn't want the whole congregation to know my business. But it was too late for that. Shame and humility went out the window again.

It's funny how life changes you. Because it has definitely changed me. I used to be so private. Now, I don't care who knows my business. It's my experience. I have nothing to prove to anybody. It's all about helping the next person who may be going through the same thing.

So, I whispered, "Yes I am sleeping in my truck". She says, "Ok, you're coming with me". I was so relieved. This lady was so excited about helping me. We need a lot of people like her in the world. God was giving me a break from this homeless experience.

We got in my truck and drove up the street to her place. She stayed in senior living (of which I didn't know at the time). We go up the stairs and open the door. There was a smell that hit my nose so hard. She had a one-bedroom apartment with 3 cats. She said her cleaning lady came but she missed that date. Well, I knew I needed a place to sleep. I knew what I had to do. Roll up my sleeves and get to cleaning. I cleaned her entire apartment except her bedroom. She didn't want me to clean her place. But I told her I didn't mind. God gave me strength to do it. She loved to talk about her son who traveled the country a lot. She kept telling me her son was going to be president one day. I wasn't sure if she was speaking things into existence (Scripture Romans 4:17) or if she had a slight mental issue. Honestly, there were a lot of people with mental issues in California.

I was blessed to stay at her place for about 1 or 2 weeks. I remember being able to park my truck at her place while I flew back home to Chicago to take a break from the journey. Then she called on the phone and told me someone had been watching me come in and out her place. She was so nice. She gave me a key to her place. She told me how she was under fixed income for her apartment and how she could get put out for having someone living there. I totally understood. So, I flew back to California. That call meant, God was telling me it was time to get back to California to live out my journey and experience. It was a pull for me to go back to this experience this time because I was extremely tired and ready for this journey to end. Going back home for a while did give me the love, push and energy I needed to continue.

I almost forgot to mention, when I came to Redondo Beach, I started looking for work. I went to different salons to find work. I met a hair product distributor in Inglewood, and he directed me to a salon in Hawthorne California. Which was only about 10 minutes from Redondo. I spoke with the owner over the phone. The lady only needed help for the weekend. She said I called at the right time because they were going to be extremely busy and needed help. But she wanted me as an assistant. I must admit, I felt some type of way about being someone's assistant. Back home in Chicago I was a Master Stylist. Meaning, I had many years of experience. I spoke with the distributor and shared with him the position the lady was offering. I told him I had been doing hair for a long time and I didn't want to be an assistant. He told me I had to start somewhere since I was new to the area. He gave me a good pep talk of which I needed. While sitting in my truck that night, the Lord spoke with me. The Lord gave me a reality check. I felt so bad and condemned. Here, a door was opening for me to make some money and because of my credentials I felt the position wasn't good enough for me. My heart felt so heavy because I knew I let an opportunity pass me. But I heard from the Lord to go work there and say to the owner, "The Lord sent me here". At this point I really needed some money. My funds had tapped out and I had no right to be picky. I came in the next day because she had previously given me the time to be at the salon. I told her what the Lord said to me and her exact words were, "I know you were God sent". She let me know I called at the right time because they had an extremely busy day planned.

Even though I had years of experience in the beauty industry, I had to humble myself.

1 Peter 5:6 says, "Humble yourselves therefore under the mighty hand of God, that he may exalt you in due time".

It turns out, I didn't only assist. She gave me my own personal clients. I was blessed to be able to shampoo and style my own hair. Because, although I had found a facility to shower. I had nowhere to do my hair and it was time for the maintenance of my hair. She paid me very well, thanked me for my help and that was it for her salon. I was hoping I could continue working there but, it turns out she only needed me for that day. This was all God's work and I was grateful. That was all the money God wanted me to have at that time, daily bread, stability.

Matthew 6:11 says, "Give us this day our daily bread". That's just what the Lord gave me.

I found a salon to work at in Redondo Beach. This salon had everything I loved. Upscale, beautifully decorated. It was painted and designed with my favorite color, purple. I met with the owner and we clicked. She was so happy to have me there and I was happy to be there. Business was a little slow but, my trust was in God that he would send the clients my way. The owner had no idea I was sleeping in my truck. I would come dressed up for work every day. I shared with her my expertise and how I was once a salon owner in Chicago. I can tell she loved her business but was exhausted because the overhead was a bit much. The location wasn't bringing in enough business. She did a lot of marketing and was very sharp at it. Working there gave me something to do during the day. I didn't make a lot of money at this salon but just enough to get by. I learned a lot about marketing through her. And built a beautiful relationship with her, even to this day. I had a beautiful experience working there.

When the senior I was living with in Redondo Beach stated I had to leave I said, "Lord where next". I could not take any more of this homelessness and sleeping in my truck. As I stated before, I was able to take a break because by going back home to Chicago, I returned refreshed and ready to get back on this journey.

So, now I'm in Redondo Beach, but I had to leave the lady's place. I was returning back but preparing myself to sleep in my truck. I remember after leaving her place I pulled over close to the beach and parked. I sat there talking to the Lord. I remember it like yesterday, it was a sunny day, I was feeling pretty good that day. I don't remember exactly how much money I had when I came back to Redondo. When I would go home to Chicago. I would do two or three special clients at my mom's place. I would occasionally let them know when I was coming into town. These clients were sowing seeds, unknowingly. They were God sent clients. They didn't know the money they paid helped me while on my journey. They may have thought I was doing them a deed, but we were helping each other.

Well, as I'm sitting there in my truck, on that beautiful sunny day. I heard the word, "Pasadena". I was so excited. For some reason in my spirit I knew this was the last part of my journey and experience of homelessness. Pasadena was the city I desired to live in.

I shared in my previous book how I went to visit Pasadena California. I thought this would be a great city for my children and I to live and experience. I smiled and thought to myself. I am headed home.

Pasadena was my final destination.

CHAPTER 11
THE PASADENA EXPERIENCE

My GPS says, "You have arrived". I arrived in Pasadena California with a smile on my face. Their city hall looks like an emperor palace. It looked like royalty. I knew this was a place for my children and I.

1Peter 2:9 says, "But ye are a chosen generation, a royal priesthood, a holy nation, a peculiar people; that ye should show forth the praises of him who hath called you out of darkness into his marvelous light".

To God be the glory. God's people are royalty, we should look at ourselves as such and be treated as such. I felt a lot stronger when I came to Pasadena. The first night I slept in my truck, but I was determined the next day to find a place to stay. There was a church near the city Hall. I always went to the church first because that's where the Holy Spirit led me and that should be the first place everyone should be able to go for help. They kept their church door wide open through the day. I thought that was such a blessing. A lot of churches keep their doors closed and locked for security reasons. It was as if they were saying, **"Come one come all; all ye that labor and are heavy laden, and I will give you rest", (Matthew 11:28).** It didn't matter your race or situation. The doors were open to come and pray or sit. Pasadena is a very rich city, but they have their share of homeless people.

I met a lady Priest at this church. I explained my situation to her, and she was willing to help me. She paid for me to stay a few nights at a hotel in Pasadena. She wrote me a referral letter to help me to get into a place called the Union Station. She said they could possibly help with housing. This place helped men and women in need. Then someone recommended another church called, "Lake Avenue". I absolutely loved this church. I met the lady who was in charge of helping people in need. I shared my spiritual journey with her. This church had a program set up to help find housing for people. Whether you were looking for a shelter or wanted to pay rent somewhere. Of course, I was not in a position to pay rent. This lady invited me out to dinner with her family the same night we met. She was very interested in this journey the Lord took me on. She was also trying to get me situated in a place to sleep. It was after hours from work with the church and her family had planned to have dinner. So, she was squeezing me in after her work schedule to help. I know this was nobody but God moving on her heart. Because she could have told me to come back tomorrow so she could spend time with her family.

She was a great example of someone with a servant's heart. She put her business to the side to help others in need. This church paid for me a hotel room for some days. Getting a bed at Union Station would take a few days so I was so grateful. She also gave me referrals. This church was very informative. I started attending church services there on Sundays. They offered a lot to the community and I wanted to be a part of that. But God had other plans.

I've learned during this journey to take one step at a time. Follow one instruction after the other. I had gone to a place called the Union Station and I explained to them my situation about not having a place to sleep. God graced and favored me. I was able to get about 10 nights at this place. They only allowed about 20 beds in this facility. This facility was used for meetings in the daytime and at night they opened the doors to those in need. They had showers and they served dinner. There were a lot of people on the list to get in this place. There was a little lady at their head office I spoke with and she became fond of me. I'm sure God used her loving heart to grant me favor and open those doors for me. I used a few of those days to go back home because I was missing my kids. I received a call from the union station, which let me know I needed to get back there, or I would lose my spot to sleep at night. So, I flew back quickly. I had to remember this was a journey of experiences. Every step in this journey would lead to something that could help and teach me in some way. I believe I missed one step when I went back home. The union station was designed to put people in permanent housing after staying at the temporary facility (Union Station) for the amount of days they allow. But I must have heard wrong, misunderstood or didn't hear at all about me receiving permanent living. So, I didn't get a permanent place to live through this program. I was so sad and beat myself down for missing that opportunity.

After living all these homeless experiences, going to different facilities, churches etc. I realized that living these experiences was like I was in training school. I saw the do and the don't. I saw how these housing facilities operated. I had to be a willing participant in these programs to see how to run these types of businesses. I collected so much paperwork. I have a heart to help the poor, those in need. God sure does have a funny way of teaching and getting the information to me.

So, I hadn't found work in Pasadena yet. I was focused on trying to put a roof over my head. As a single woman the government was giving me a really hard time with getting help. I was in tears. Part of me wanted to go back home but I hadn't heard from the Lord to leave. The Union station had given me a list of shelters in LA, and surrounding cities but I clearly heard the Lord say Pasadena. I would not go outside the boundaries of Pasadena. I knew it was my safe-haven and God wanted me here for a purpose. So, while going to these places to get help, one place spoke to me about receiving government assistance. They asked if I had kids. I could get help with food, cash and medical. I didn't want to get on government assistance but, this was the route I was being taken on. I'm thinking, Lord have mercy on me. I could not believe this was the route I was getting ready to take. It seemed the only way I would get help quickly was with kids. I'm thinking, "I have kids". They are not here with me, but I have kids. So, I said, "Yes".

Now, the Holy Spirit had already put in my heart that my son needed me. My daughter missed me, but she was doing fine. She had her dad, cousins and friends back home, so she was enjoying herself. My son was more to himself. He only had me as a parent. I mentioned in my previous book his dad died. That was a void in his heart. He didn't have many male figures to step in and help. But he had God as his father and me to guide him along the way. I must admit as of today he has turned out to be a very respectable young man.

I knew in my heart; my son was ready to see me daily. I think I have been on this journey of experiences for about 4 months. My kids had never been apart from me for such an extended time. Bringing them to California at that time would require me to take them out of class in the middle of the school year. My children had always been excited about California because moving there was our dream. But I'd much rather been financially situated before moving them there but, God had a plan.

Here I am a woman who was once financially stable, a giver, a person with a good heart, healthy, once a business and homeowner and now on public assistance. But at this point, I didn't care. I had to get on assistance to get all the help I needed. California was expensive like Chicago. I explained to my kids this help was temporary. They did not care. They were two happy kids in California. Being on public assistance helped with putting the kids in school. They gave out vouchers to help with school supplies. It helped with food, medical and housing. The government gave me vouchers for a hotel room, until that ran out. I had been looking for an apartment. But when the voucher for the hotel ran out, I then used the cash the state gave me to pay for the hotel rooms. These hotel rooms were expensive. We stayed at just about every hotel on Colorado Boulevard in Pasadena. I always tried to find good rates for weeks at a time. Most people would look at this situation as a sad time, but it was not for us. We had a roof over our head. Staying at a hotel was nice. My kids were enjoying themselves. It was if we were living a life of luxury. Here we had nice hotels, cleaning service, pool, and a fitness room. It was not a sad moment. It was truly a blessing. But then the hotel fees were beginning to be a bit much because my funds were getting low.

Then that special day for many Americans came around, "Tax Season". I thought, "God always knows when to show up". I wanted to use that money for the apartment. I found a one-bedroom apartment, it was very spacious and nice. The kids were very excited about the pool. Although, I had to get approved for the apartment. Spring break approached so we were able to go home to Chicago. We were in prayer for this apartment because we needed a place to live when school started back. I remember the landlord calling and approving me for the apartment. I was still in Chicago at the time. I had the tax money in my account as an act of good faith to show the landlord. I hadn't found work, but I was still looking, so I honestly didn't know how I was going to pay the rent after a few months. I let him know I was a hairstylist, and I would be starting work soon. That's what I was believing God for. He said, "Ok". I know this was nothing but the favor of God getting me in this apartment. The average landlord would have wanted more proof of income. So, I had to hurry back to California and meet with the landlord to sign the lease because spring break was ending, and school would be starting soon. I took care of all the paperwork, then I sent for the kids to come. We were extremely excited to be in this place. I was still looking for a salon to work at. I went to an interview with one salon, but it was not a good fit for me.

    The school year was coming to an end and my tax money was running out. The rent date had approached. Still no work. Since I did not know what our living situation would be I sent the kids back to Chicago for the summer while I figured things out. I was not going to have my kids sleeping in the truck (if this was going to happen). I did not believe that was part of God's plan. Thank God I never had to sleep in my truck again after the first day of being in Pasadena. I must admit, I felt off track in this part of my journey. I needed to be alone so I could hear from God and figure things out.

I had nowhere or no one to get the rent from. I did not like asking for help. I prefer to be the giver. Besides, I really did not have many who could help to pay my rent. I was on a journey of which not many would understand, so I did not want to ask help from anyone that would question my journey. It's crazy, but when you ask family for help many tend to think the worst. They talk about you behind your back and question why you are in the situation you are in instead of just helping. I can only assume my family was used to me being on top financially but didn't understand what was going on. I say, just help and do what you can. Stop trying to question everything. Give what you can give. It takes a lot of nerve to ask for help. I believe, if a person asks for help, they must really need it.

I know God speaks to people and gives them instructions. Because I am one of those people. I hear and obey (at least to the best of my ability). So, I thought the Lord would do the same to help me along this journey. I remember when my cell bill was due it was almost two months behind. I didn't know how it would get paid. Then the Lord put it on my heart to call a friend and ask her to pay my phone bill. I worked up the nerves to call and ask. She said she would see what she could do. She mentioned she would have to try and move some money around and she would call me back. I didn't get a yes or no and that made me feel a little disappointed. I was thinking Lord, why would you have me call her, for her to act like she didn't have the money to pay my bill.

But I patiently waited on her call. As she said, she moved some money around and found a way. God already knew she had it or he wouldn't have told me to call her. She paid the bill. I was grateful to God but, I felt some type of way afterwards because I didn't feel like she was ok with helping me. I hate for people to think I need them, and I don't like feeling like I owe them. Not to say she would but, I just did not like how I felt after she paid the bill.

So, the next day she called and said she had something to share with me. I said, "Ok, what". She said she already knew she was supposed to give me some money. She heard the Lord tell her to give me some money one month ago. But she didn't obey. God always blesses her with more than enough and she knows this as well. I was glad she called and was honest with me. Because it confirmed what I heard in my spirit for her to assist me. And it confirmed why I felt that uneasy feeling inside after she gave me the money. I thanked her for calling me back and being honest. Her honesty gave me ease. Discernment is a tool and it never fails. Obedience is key and it never fails.

Luke 6:38 says, "Give and it shall be given unto you; good measure pressed down, and shaken together, and running over, shall men give into your bosom. For with the same measure that you give, it shall be measured to you again.

CHAPTER 12
THE HEART AND SOUL OF A REALTOR

While living in my apartment I met this older man who was a realtor. He wanted me to get into Real Estate with him. Real Estate was something I always wanted to do. We became cool. It seemed he hadn't been in the Real Estate business for a while and he was trying to get back in it. We sat down one day for lunch. I mentioned I was looking for work as a hairstylist. He said the barbershop he goes to may be hiring. It was a unisex salon. So, he gave me the contact information. While sitting there we talked about lots of things. Somehow, we got on the topic of God and faith. He told me he didn't believe there was a heaven or hell. He hadn't accepted Jesus Christ as his Lord and Savior. We talked about our spirituality. He was also trying to help me find somewhere to live. I had shared with him I would have to leave my apartment by a certain date. (During this time, as I mentioned, I sent my kids back home for the summer and they would return when school started back in August). While they were gone, I had gone to court and was given a date I would have to leave the apartment. The landlord was a nice senior. He told me he understood my situation and what I was going through and hoped something worked out for me. He did not put an eviction on my record.

It was time for me to vacate the apartment. So, the realtor suggested I stay with him for a little while, since I had nowhere to go. Before he made the suggestion, the Lord had already confirmed with me to stay with him, as my next move but, I didn't make mention of this to him. Even though I knew in my spirit, I still had to wait until the realtor said something. This was something I learned during my journey as I walked by faith. I was truly excited because I did not want to sleep in my truck ever again. I was finally in Pasadena (which was my final destination), I knew the experience of homelessness was over.

I had never been inside his place. So, I walked in not knowing what to expect. What a total surprise, it was an estimated 12X10 space. No exaggeration. As soon as you walk in, you see the twin size bed and his music studio (he played the guitar). On the left was a wall that separated the bed area from the toilet, a tiny shower and a tiny kitchen. There was a curtain that separated the kitchen and toilet area from the bed. If I can remember, I lost my breath when I walked in because I was in total shock. I told him to give me a few minutes. I stepped outside and sat in my truck and started praying in tongues. I'm thinking Lord, "How are two grown people going to sleep in this space". This was a man who stood about 6"4" in height.

I shook off what I was feeling because this was a part of God's plan. I went back inside. And I said, "Ok, I prayed, and I will stay, thank you". As I took a good look at the place, I noticed it needed cleaning. I told him I was going to clean the place for him. I often joked with my mom and my spiritual friend back home saying I was the cleanup lady in California. It seemed everywhere I went I had to clean.

He said he would sleep on the floor and give me the bed. That was so polite of him. This place was so tiny he would not have enough room to sleep on the floor. He had things everywhere. I took nothing out of my truck but my bible and purse. Only in the morning when it was time to get dressed, did I pull my clothes out of the truck. He was an older man, I didn't want to put him on the floor, so I told him he could sleep at the foot and I would sleep at the head of the twin size bed. I appreciated him opening his doors to me. He was respectable. He would leave when it was time for me to get dressed. If he was thinking about approaching me the wrong way, he never acted on it and I am so grateful to God for that.

During my few days I was living with him we prayed, and I shared the love and word of God with him. Days passed and that space was just too tight for the both of us. But my spirit let me know that I was not to leave until he asked me to leave. I believe that gave me time to share the love of God with him.

One day he said, "It's becoming too tight in here" and he asked me to leave. I had already known that exit was coming. Remember, my spirit had warned me, my time of ministering to him was up. So, the Lord gave me one final message to share with him. The message was, "The Lord is concerned about your soul and where you are going to spend eternity". I remember he smiled, received the message and thanked me. I thanked him for allowing me to stay and left. Weeks passed and I hadn't heard from him. So, I went by his place to check on him. The neighbors said he had a stroke or a heart attack (I can't remember which one exactly). He was in his apartment when it happened. She said he had been in there for 2 days and nobody knew. She said they took him to the hospital, and he was in a bad condition. I went to the local hospital to visit him, but he was not there. They said his son took him out of that hospital because he wanted his dad in a hospital closer to him. The neighbor gave me the son's phone number. I don't remember talking to him, so I never knew his full condition. I never heard from the realtor ever again. I often wonder if he's still alive.

The barber who cuts the realtor hair worked at the same salon as me. I told him what happened with the realtor and I told him how he helped me and allowed me to sleep a few nights at his place before his sickness. The barber says, "You know he likes to sleep with young girls, like you". He mentioned how the realtor would share his stories about the young girls he slept with him. I said well he never tried with me. He said, "Well you better thank God". His barber was a preacher in Pasadena.

Psalm 91:10 says, "No evil shall come near my dwelling".

God kept me protected around that older realtor man. I was under the instructions of the Lord. Which means I was covered by the blood. Sometimes the Lord will send you into dark places when living this life of faith.

I had to trust In the Lord with all my heart, (Proverbs 3:5,6). Psalm 23:4 says, "Yea though I walk through the valley of the shadow of death, I will fear no evil: for thou art with me; thy rod and thy staff they comfort me."
Psalm 91:2 says, "I will say of the Lord, He is my refuge and my fortress: my God; in him will I trust".

God protects and keeps us from danger especially when we are on assignment. I had an assignment to complete with that realtor. My assignment was to talk to him about the Lord and how He was concerned about where he would spend eternity. After leaving him, I'm not sure if he accepted Christ as his Lord and Savior. I can only hope and pray he did.

CHAPTER 13
JUST IN TIME

When I first met the realtor and I told him I was looking for work. I shared with you how he wanted me to do Real Estate with him. But I needed money right away. He told me about the barbershop/salon where he went to get his haircut. I called and met with the owner. He asked, "When would I like to start. I said, "Tomorrow". Business was slow for the hairstylist. It was a well-known salon/barbershop in Pasadena, so I was trusting God that word would spread about the new stylist from Chicago. All I needed was to get my hands on a couple of clients and the word would spread. The owner was known for helping many out of town stylists and barbers, along with people in his community. By the time I started working at this salon, I was being put out of my apartment because I could not pay the rent. I asked the landlord if he could use my deposit to pay the present rent, then I would be able to pay rent after that since I had finally started working. None of my reasoning worked. I was not mad at him. I totally understood. That apartment lasted as long as I needed it to last me. So, I was thankful. I had a court order to leave and I was glad I did not have an eviction on me. God covered me. The landlord and his attorney were really nice about everything. I believe this man knew I was not being dishonest with him. I was new to the area and in hope of starting a new life here and he wanted to give me a chance.

Well, I left the apartment. And as I mentioned, I stayed with the realtor for a few days until it was time to leave his place. The owner of the salon knew my situation and paid for many of my hotel stays. During this journey I have learned outside people (people who are not your family) will sometimes help, support and aid you quicker than family. He told me he wanted to help me and knew this the minute we sat and conversated. He said he saw potential. I was glad because I needed the opportunity. It was hard finding an apartment in Pasadena. The owner wanted to help me keep the apartment I was living in but I was about 1 week too late of meeting him. I had already gone to court and had to vacate. I was so sad. I really liked that apartment, and the price was right. I knew once I started making money, I would be able to afford it. I found out perhaps that was not a part of God's plan. It was a temporary fix for my situation. I had to get back on track. I found out later in my journey, the apartment was never a part of God's plan. God graced me for that time period.

CHAPTER 14
THE SLIGHT MISSED OPPORTUNITY

Well, I had been working in the salon for about one month. I was making money but not enough to afford an apartment. I had been looking for rooms to rent or another big one bedroom for cheap. The owner of the salon had been paying for me to stay at hotels. If I had a good week, I would pay for my own stay, but he always helped me.

Before I sent myself through the frustration of finding an apartment for my kids and I, I looked into this transitional housing program called, "Door of Hope". I met with the people and they had a brand-new home they were opening. The administrator said we would be the first family to move in. I don't know what happened but, somehow, I misunderstood that I was to call them back. Unfortunately, I missed my date for the next step to get in the program so we could move in. I would have had a place for the kids and I to live when they first came to California and I screwed that up. I did not realize that, until later down the journey. That is why we were going from hotel to hotel and had to get that apartment.

That's why I say it's ok to make mistakes in your journey. We learn from them. But just know, God still provides in the process. Meanwhile I was still at the hotel and school was getting ready to start. It was time to send the kids back to Cali again. I finally worked up the nerve to ask my stepdad for hotel money since I had the kids with me. I didn't want to ask for help when it was just me. He was one of the people I could have gone to for help. The Lord did not put him on my heart at the time to ask. He sent the money with no questions. I explained to him we were waiting for a place to call that would provide housing for us and I let him know we were ok.

We stayed at most of the hotels along Colorado Boulevard in Pasadena. Business was going well at the salon, so I no longer needed help from the owner for hotels. But it would sometimes have its slow weeks. One day I didn't have the money for the hotel, again. This time I was tired of trying to figure things out. So, I parked, and we sat in the truck. My daughter was chilling in the back seat and my son had kicked off his shoes as if he were preparing to sleep in the truck. I remember we all started laughing when my son kicked off his shoes. We found laughter and made a joke out of everything. We knew we were in this together.

While sitting, the thought of this Pasadena Pastor came to mind. An associate in California spoke about him to me previously. So, I called and asked her for his number. He opened his couches to us. We walked in his place. The kids and I were relieved we didn't have to sleep in the truck. I didn't want my kids to experience sleeping in a vehicle. I was humbly grateful to have met this Pastor. I was hoping this Pastor could help find a house for my children and I. He would always say you need a house for you and your children. It seemed he had resources. But none of them worked for me. So, I had to be thankful for the help he was able to give, which was the couches and a place to shower.

I called Door of Hope (the housing program) because I remembered I hadn't heard back from them. I wanted to know what happened with my kids and I being accepted into this program. Remember, I mentioned I was supposed to call this transitional housing for families back, because they were ready to move the kids and I into the new home. But I made the mistake of not hearing and following directions. While on the phone, they explained to me I never called them back to get admitted. But they did let me know they did have a room available and would call me back. At this point school had started. We stayed at the Pastor's place for about 7 days. Door of Hope called me back on the 3rd day of being at the Pastors place. This was such a blessing. I did a phone interview, and they confirmed my stay, again. We moved into this clean, new and beautiful home. I thanked the Pastor and we stayed connected. Meeting this Pastor was a Divine connection from God.

CHAPTER 15
THE DOOR OF HOPE EXPERIENCE

The kids and I were grateful to have had a couch to sleep on before the Door of Hope called but, we were ready to go back to sleeping in beds and being organized. Because we had all our belongings in the truck. We were riding like sardines in a jar (full). I remember us walking into Door of Hope. It was a two-story home, big and beautiful. They took us upstairs to show us our very own room. We saw 4 bunk beds and were excited. It was nice and roomy, 2 bathrooms upstairs, full kitchen, washer and dryer. We had everything we needed in this house.

Door of Hope is a program designed to help all families in need. This program was faith based and had many rules to follow as well as curfew. I learned a lot from this program as well. They helped with finding housing beyond Door of Hope, teaching families how to save money, pushed you to find work, helped with the kids and when holidays came, they really shower the families with gifts. They had many companies and organizations that sponsored their program. They made a great impact in the Pasadena community. Although they offered a lot, we didn't ask for much, we just needed a roof over our heads.

Our lives were a different story coming into this program than others. We were in need but not totally in need. We were never to come into this program with a poor or needy mentality. Even though the situation looked the way it did. The Lord always told me, "It's not what it looks like". We were never to have a poverty mindset. This was a learning experience for us, and I knew the Lord opened these doors for my children and I. We had a roof over our head but, I was also learning the dos and don'ts of running a transitional housing program for families.

Although it was a roof over our head, as months passed my children were getting frustrated with the rules and living in a house with other families.

There would be days I had to work late and was unable to pick my children up from school, so they had to take public transportation. They did not like that because when it was time for the bus to stop by our block, there were kids they knew that got off as well. Being seen walking into Door of Hope was embarrassing for them. The funny part is my kids would rush ahead of the other kids because they didn't want them to see where they live. They told me they would act like they were racing each other to the house so they could be way ahead of the other kids. They would have been fine if the house hadn't had such a big sign on it, that said, "Door of Hope". We laughed so hard about it.

I know someone reading this may be feeling sorry for us but, don't. My kids and I always made light of situations that may have been sad to others. We love to laugh and joke. This always kept us strong, encouraged and motivated to keep moving. Besides, this was an experience for us.

Some of the house rules didn't make sense so, of course, I spoke my mind because I didn't agree with all of them. I speak my mind a lot when change is needed. I am a change agent, an atmosphere shaker. Things change for the better when I walk in a room. To God be the glory. This is the way all kingdom believers should live.

They changed many of the rules I addressed. I remember the Lord telling me to open my mouth about what I didn't like because my voice could make a change. These rules didn't only give my kids ease but helped other families in the house as well. It was hard to go to work, come home and then have all these rules to abide to. I felt we were not living a life of freedom. I always stood on this one scripture that speaks about freedom.

2Corinthians 3:17, "Where the Spirit of the Lord is, there is freedom (liberty)".

I remember sharing scriptures with some of the staff of the house. The lack of freedom was bringing a dark cloud over my children and I knew this was not a part of God's plan. This experience was a little devastating at times for them, but I didn't want them to lose their happiness, joy and laughter.

I would take them to Beverly Hills, and we would go to open houses looking at big, beautiful homes. I wanted to keep their imaginations going because the word of God says, **"Wealth and**

Riches are in their houses, and their righteousness endures forever", Psalm112:3.

I wanted my children to know this is the type of life God wants us to have. The blessed life. Financially, I would have some good weeks at the salon. So, I was still able to show them a good time and good living. We were not poor, even though our living situation looked that way because we didn't have our own place. Unfortunately, there were some families whose lives did take a bad turn. There were women with children in this house who needed a boost to save money to get their life back on track. These were working moms but were in a transitional part of their lives and needed a little help. Many of the families were not happy to be there, especially those of us who had teenagers. The teenagers were hard to please. It was embarrassing for them. They were in high school and these were supposed to be the best years of their life, but they were being restricted because of life turns. The little kids had no idea what was going on. They were happy little butterflies around the house. This was a teaching experience for my kids. They have always been fortunate. They were able to see what many families go through. They were about to see the hard knocks life can bring. This experience made them very appreciative.

Eventually our time was running out with Door of Hope and we would need to leave. We had certain obligations and dates we had to abide to when it came to submitting paperwork. The issue they had with me was they wanted me to get a punch the clock job. That didn't work for me. I had been an entrepreneur for a long time and working the 9-5 jobs they wanted me to work was not going to pay me the amount of money I could make as a hairstylist. This was another rule I tried changing with them. Teaching them about self-employment, entrepreneurship. They didn't think it was a stable job because as hair stylists we don't make the same amount of money every week. They felt I needed a consistent check. I let them know being a hairstylist is a job. They didn't like us being paid in cash because they needed to keep track of what we were making, of which I understood. Their way of keeping track was seeing everyone's pay stubs or direct deposit. This was a pretty good system. They allowed me to work at a salon as a hairstylist. Weekly I would report how much I made. But their rule was for me to go find a job with a consistent check. I went on a couple of interviews and it never worked. Many of these companies wanted you to attend classes before you worked for them. It was such a waste of my time and I would only get paid minimum wage. That was not God's best for me at that time. I was on a journey of experiences and I knew to keep my freedom. I learned a lot about the system of this world and about Corporate America. I had no idea. I had been self-employed for so long I was blind to how things work in the Corporate world. You have to jump through so many hoops just to get the job.

I followed the program rules and reported every interview I went on. But every time I didn't find a job, I had to get a write up. If you received three write ups, you would not be able to receive the money they give you to help you move into your apartment (once you found a place). I had two write ups. They gave each family about 5 months to get our life together by getting a job and saving money. I understood what they were doing as far as pushing people to make it out here in life.

I had been looking for an apartment for my kids and I to live in because I knew we were going to have to move eventually. My exit date was approaching, and I hadn't found a place for me and my kids. I remember one of the housing directors telling me I would need to hurry and find something. He didn't believe I would find anything with the amount of days I had left to be in the program. I was trying to beat the date they gave me to move and not get put out of the program because I hadn't found a punch the clock job, which would have been my third strike. I spoke these words out of my mouth to the housing director, "The Lord is going to find us a place, watch and see". I told him, "I am a woman of great faith". He smiled and shook his head. Now, this program I was in was a faith-based program. But what the Lord showed me was that this director's faith was not at my level. They worked the program, prayed with families, helped many families and loved the people as the word of God says. But living a life of faith was something different. And so, I was to be a walking, talking and living example of faith.

Well, the Pastor I met in Pasadena, who opened his couches to us, told me about an apartment above his church. I wasn't too sure about moving there. But, then after giving it some thought, I said this would be a great idea. I didn't have much time to waste anyway. The Pastor had trusted his keys to the church with me after we'd gotten to know each other. He allowed me to go there to pray and intercede whenever I wanted. So, being upstairs from the church was wonderful. I would go down there any time of the day.

CHAPTER 16
HALLELUJAH WE ARE FREE

When we moved into this apartment the kids and I were so happy to have our independence back. Our life had taken such a drastic turn. Who would have known this would happen? Now, we were ready to live the California life. Even though we were living this humbling experience, I always loved California. It was like waking up to a vacation every day. The beautiful palm trees and the sun. Even on a bad day it was a good day because it was so beautiful.

When we were in the Door of Hope program, public housing opened. Door of Hope had all the parents fill out the forms so we could get on the list. I had never done anything like this before. I was nervous and excited at the same time. I always heard about the program and how cheap the rent would be. I felt this was a blessing as well. We had been living in our apartment. I was paying regular rent (no help from the government).

I found out when you are in a shelter with kids, public housing moves much quicker for you. They move your name up the list. This was good for us. Although we were on our own. I was renting bedrooms from this apartment. So, it was still a shared space with one other person. It was like we had the place to ourselves because she always stayed in her room. The kids and I really enjoyed being there. The Landlord was really nice.

Now that I was living on my own, I had more freedom to do more things at night. I could stay places later than normal. I was a part of a network marketing company and there was always something going on. At times I could not attend because I had curfew at Door of Hope.

The Pastor and I met often to sit and talk. He would always be delighted to hear about my journey. I shared everything with him. He was glad to see a woman, young and of great faith. I would attend his church sometime.

Once he got comfortable with me, he gave me a copy of the keys to his church (As I mentioned). He wanted me to go there as often as I liked. He wanted me to pray for the church, city, and anything the Lord put in my spirit. When I was living at Door of Hope, I could not pray as loud as I needed. I did not have the quiet time and space that I was used to having. So, I remember sharing that with him and that is when he offered the keys to the church. Getting the keys to a church was something that had never happened to me. I felt like God himself stood over me and gifted me something so valuable and I would guard it with my life. I have total respect for the house of the Lord. Sometimes I would leave the salon in the middle of the day, go over to the church, turn on my music, worship and pray. In those times of prayer, the Holy Spirit would speak to me about many things. My steps were being ordered by the Lord. **Psalm 37:23, "The steps of a good man are ordered by the Lord".**

It was good to have someplace quiet to go when chaos is all around you. When in worship one should be able to be free and loud as ever. I often pray in tongues and the Lord would reveal things to me afterwards. I remember the Lord revealing to me to gather women in prayer. I was to invite women to the church for a gathering of prayer. It was a wonderful experience. The Lord had shown me a lot that was happening in Pasadena especially with leadership in the churches and how the city needed a Holy Spirit sweep through. Many were going to church but there was no presence of the Holy Spirit/the Lord. I really wanted to be a part of whatever God was going to do in that city.

CHAPTER 17
A CALL TO MINISTRY

I went to the church one day to pray alone. I was thanking God and giving praises to him. I was on my knees in the pulpit and I heard the words, "Minister, Pastor is to ordain you as a Minister". Honestly, I rejected what I heard. I was crying so hard. This was not something I expected or what I wanted. The life I was living in faith showed that my life could be leading to this position but, I just never saw it for myself. When I shared this news with my family and a few friends they were not surprised. Some said why are you surprised. They knew it was leading up to this. Even my mom knew it was coming. I never thought I would be called to ministry as a minister. I battled with what the Lord shared with me. I sat on the floor of the church for about one hour, crying. My eyes were red. At the time, I felt being a Minister was too much of a responsibility and I did not want that type of pressure on me. The name "Minister" carried weight and pressure. I felt my life would change drastically. I must be honest; I did not want to be associated with the name preacher. I could not see being called a Minister.

I remember calling my spiritual friend back home. I was very hesitant on the phone with her about sharing what the Lord had spoken to me. I always felt like she should have been the one to be called to preach. She is very good with memorizing scriptures and I felt as a preacher you had to memorize the whole bible. My memory was not as good. Of course, it takes more than just memorizing scriptures to preach. And for whatever reason God saw it in me.

My spiritual friend and I are on the phone. I was trying to get the words out as I was crying. She is on the phone asking me what's wrong. After hesitating I finally cry the word, "Minister". I shared with her I was at the church and how the Lord is calling me to be a Minister and how the Pastor is to ordain me. She talked me through the ordeal by giving me words of comfort. The word ordain is something serious and not to be played with. That is why I was taking it so hard. I felt I was being held to a standard with God. He would be expecting things to happen through me as he used me for His glory. I knew with me being ordained there were some things that I could not do anymore because I would be wearing the name Minister. I did not want people looking or treating me different. Sometimes I can over think things, which is not good which is what I did in this case. I remember the Lord saying to me why should I do anything for you, and you will not obey me. Those words hit my heart. I pulled myself together.

I had spoken with the Pastor of the church earlier and he told me he would meet me at the church later that day. So, I was expecting him to show up that evening while I was present at the church. He came and sat in the already saturated atmosphere of the church. He had his prayer time and then we went into the fellowship room to talk. He and I would meet often. We were sitting there; he was doing most of the talking. I was still kind of numb, shocked and quiet. He knew something was going on. I remember the Pastor asking me if there was something, I wanted to share with him. Even though I'd surrendered to God to obey what He said. I was not ready to share this with the Pastor. It was so hard to get the word Minister out of my mouth. He kept pulling at me by having me go to the bible and find scriptures and recite them. He had a way with getting people to talk. He always called me his tough one. Because I didn't like to talk much. I often let him do much of the talking. I'm more of an analyzer. When we would meet for our class sessions, the Lord would often give me a message for him. We often encouraged each other. Iron sharpens iron. Unknowingly the Lord sent me as a Ministering Prophet to him. The Lord would reveal a message to me about him, for him and I would relay it to him. Pastor was very thankful. When he first met me, he told me there was something different about me, but he hadn't figured it out. From the outside I had that Chicago swag but, on the inside, I was so full of the Spirit of God. When I opened my mouth to speak the word of God, the Holy Spirit inside of me would take over. Whatever the Lord led me to speak, it would be a confirmation for him.

As we'd gotten to know each other, I believe the Lord revealed to him what was so different about me. It was the presence of the Lord inside of me. He started seeing me differently. Seeing me fully through the eyes of God. He then knew I had been set aside to be used for God's glory.

So, finally I told him I am hearing the Lord say you are to ordain me as a Minister. He says, "I already know". He was waiting on me. He said he had known this for a while. His words were, "But you are so tough, I had to wait for you to get it".

Before getting to know this Pastor, I remember the Lord sending me to his church and I was supposed to attend it on a regular basis. I will admit, I did not obey because, in my eyes it didn't look like part of the plan. This was a tiny old school church. Back home I attended a pretty large congregation. Mind you I didn't know what God's plan was when I met him. Before meeting the Pastor and before my kids came, I was attending a different church. When my kids came to California, I took them to the church I had been attending and they enjoyed it. I brought them with me to visit the Pastor church once and I knew they would prefer the other church. For their sake I attended the other church on a regular basis. I had a Holy Spirit awakening. The Lord revealed to me this was not about what the kids wanted. The Lord was building a relationship with the Pastor and I. The Lord had a plan from the very beginning. I just needed to hear and obey.

Us meeting was divinely done by God. The Holy Spirit let me know to go back and attend the Pastor's church. We met on a regular basis reading and studying the word. Before finding out the Pastor would ordain me, he told me we needed to meet a few times a week to study. I believe this is something the Lord was assigning him to do. I enjoyed studying the Bible. Unknowingly, I was in school of ministry and I was in preparation to be ordained. We were in session for months.

The Lord sent me all the way to California to be ordained as a Minister. The Lord already knew the person he was going to use to ordain me. The Lord knew the time and season He wanted me ordained.

God always has a plan. There is always strategy to His plan. We may expect it to look and operate one way. But I have learned, God's way is best.

CHAPTER 18
ORDINATION

Well, my day of ordination had arrived. I finished my time of ministry school. So, I had my mom come to town, my kids and the congregation were there to support me. The Pastor wanted to have this big ordination. He wanted to invite Pastors from all over. He wanted to have it at a church bigger than his. He was so excited for me. He would always tell me that I would go far in life. He wanted me to preach the gospel all over the world. He loved to hear me speak. So, he wanted everyone to know me. With him wanting to make my ordination a big deal, he wanted to switch it to a later date. But I told him, no because I was not hearing that in my Spirit. The Lord had been putting an urgency in me, for some reason. This ordination needed to happen soon. So, I shared it with him, and he was ok with it. I don't really like a lot of attention on me. That is one of the reasons I couldn't understand why God ordained me to preach. I don't like talking in front of a crowd. I get so nervous. I'm really a private person. But God knows what's on the inside of me. Once I start talking about the word of God, I get so full inside and I then allow the Holy Spirit to go to work by using me.

I was so nervous during the ordination. I must be honest I was still not fully persuaded that I should be a Minister. Yet, this was happening. I surrendered to the call, but I hadn't fully accepted in my mind. So, I went through the process. Before getting ordained, I remember the Pastor sitting me down and saying to me, "Do you know what you are getting into". He gave the good points as to becoming a Minister, but then he mentioned the sad points. He mentioned how lonely it can be as a preacher, especially since I was single. He named the list of things he did as a Pastor and how tiring it can be. He talked about certain things he couldn't do as a Pastor anymore. I listened to him give the list, but the fact of the matter was, I was called by God to be an ordained Minister and I just wanted to obey. Everything he mentioned was enough to scare me away from the call God had on my life, but I could not and would not walk away. My journey was all about hearing and obeying. The celebration was fun. Everyone congratulated me. We ate and laughed. I greatly appreciated everyone who showed up.

CHAPTER 19
BYE BYE CALI, SWEET HOME CHICAGO

I had a dream which let me know it was time to leave California. But I did not want to believe it. Surely God didn't want me to leave the beautiful California. Leaving California was not a thought in my mind. Not with all I had endured. I knew my start was rough, but I was ready to tough it out. I used to have a shirt I loved to wear. It said, "Tough Cookie". That is who I am. So, I was willing to ride the bumpy road to survive in California because I knew that bumpy road would lead to paradise. So, I ignored that dream of which God was instructing me to leave.

I was now an ordained Minister. Which was a new and unfamiliar chapter in my life. Shortly after being ordained I went through an awkward phase. I remember feeling a certain way that I couldn't understand. I started looking different to myself. I wanted to make changes to my hair, so I did. That didn't help what I was feeling inside. I went to the church of which the Pastor gave me access to, and I prayed. I sat there worshipping and meditating. In my time of worship, I clearly heard the words, "It's time to go". It was brought to my remembrance a second dream that let me know it was time to go. As I mentioned, the first dream I had I ignored, which was to leave California. The second dream I knew for sure it was time to go. The Lord showed me destruction in the dream. I shared the dream with my spiritual Aunt. She confirmed what God was revealing to me. So, it was time to leave the beautiful California. There was a Holy Spirit fear that came upon me after that dream. I was really sad to have to leave California. I had connected with some beautiful people. I didn't know how to tell them I would be leaving to go back to Chicago. Especially the salon owner and the Pastor. I prayed and the Lord gave me what to say to them. Which was, I am being led by the Holy One to go back home. It's time for me to leave.

The Lord gave me step by step instructions of how to get back home because we had so many belongings we had accumulated. I did not want to drive back through the mountains and hills. As I mentioned that was a very scary ride to California. The Lord put on my heart to call a family friend that would drive for me. He agreed and so we loaded up the truck and we moved back to Chicago. That was the end of my California experience.

Back in Chicago, at this point in my journey I was hurt, shocked and a little lost because returning to Chicago was not part of my plan. I was happy for my kids because they were excited to come back home. I felt like I left a part of me behind. I felt incomplete. Many days I cried to God asking why he would have me to go through all I went through, to return back home. I wondered why he wouldn't allow me to live there. But the Lord told me He had work for me to do back in Chicago. There were people waiting on me. He was sending me to reach, teach and connect with people for His glory. After hearing this answer from God, I finally accepted God's will for me in my hometown as well as California. So, I said to California, "Until we meet again". It's not about my plan, but God's plan.

ENCOURAGEMENT FOR GOD'S BELOVED

I speak of hearing and obeying often in this book because this is a way of life I've been called into. I desire for God to direct my path. It's not easy but God wants us to live a life led by the Holy Spirit.

God knows what we are made of and He knows our strengths and weaknesses. He wouldn't give us an instruction if He didn't think we couldn't finish the assignment. So, if God is instructing you to do something that looks and sounds scary, trust the plan. Not your plan but God's plan. You don't know what's attached to it.

You never know why the Lord sends you somewhere and you don't know who it's for. Be led by the Spirit of God. Follow your instinct. Someone may need you, even from a distance.

As we go through our life journey. We should learn something from each experience.

CONNECT WITH ME ACROSS SOCIAL MEDIA PLATFORMS

INSTAGRAM @fatimalatacha_faithsister

FACEBOOK @faithsister

YOUTUBE @Fatima LaTacha

WWW.FATIMALMASSEY.COM

www.ingramcontent.com/pod-product-compliance
Lightning Source LLC
Chambersburg PA
CBHW071854070526
44583CB00016B/1683